James Jesus Angleton: Was He Right?

By Edward Jay Epstein

A Short-form Book

Published by FastTrack Press/ EJE Publications, Ltd.
New York, New York
Copyright © by EJE Publication 2011, 2013 All Rights Reserved
ISBN 978-1495203473

Book Design and Photography by Ines and Ena Talakic
www.inesandena.com

Revised, January 15, 2014

For Sir James Goldsmith

Contents

Prologue　　THE FUNERAL OF A MIND　　9

Part One　　DOWN THE RABBIT HOLE　　11

    1.　Flowers of Deception
    2.　The Trust
    3.　The Desert
    4.　The Incubus
    5.　Bagley's Story

Part Two　　THE UNIVERSE OF DECEPTION

    6.　The Espionage Business
    7.　Kim and Jim
    8.　Theory of Perfect Deception
    9.　Enter Golitsyn
    10.　The Cuban Warning

Part Three   THE FALL OF ANGLETON

        11.   *The White Feather*
        12.   *The Fisherman*

Part Four   THE ASSESSMENT

        13.   *The Mole Question*
        14.   *The Deception Question*
        15.   *R.I.P*

Appendix   COLD WAR SPIES

        I.   *The War of Shadows*
        II.   *The Spy Who Came Back From The Dead*
        III.   *The Ames Postscript*
        IV.   *The Bagley Reprise*

Prologue

THE FUNERAL OF A MIND WARRIOR

On May 14, 1987, some of the most powerful men in Washington, including senators, ambassadors, cabinet officers, generals, and two former directors of Central intelligence, gathered in a small church in Arlington, Virginia to pay their last respects to James Jesus Angleton. The only decoration was a wreath of giant purple orchids, sent by Angleton's former comrades in the OSS, the organization where forty-four years earlier he had begun his career as a spy. Few words were spoken, nor needed to be. The poem "Gerontion," written by his friend T. S. Eliot and read at the service, perfectly described his quest. It describes a blind man's journey through a "wilderness of mirrors," a journey very much like Angleton's effort to find his way through the labyrinth of deception in the Cold War. The service for the poet-spy was over in less than forty minutes.

Most of those attending the service were familiar with Angleton's extraordinary career. He was born on December 9, 1917 in Boise, Idaho, the same year as the Russian Revolution. His father, James Hugh Angleton, had been a cavalry officer in the Idaho National Guard who had met his mother, Carmen Mercedes Moreno, on a military expedition to Mexico. She was only seventeen year old when they married. She gave her son a common Mexican middle name, Jesus. Fifteen years later, his father bought the Italian franchise for the National Cash Register Company, and moved his family to Milan Italy. Angleton then went to Malvern College in England before going to Yale in 1937. There, together with his roommate Reed Whittemore, he founded and edited Furioso, a quarterly devoted to original poetry. Through it, he published such leading poets as Ezra Pound, Archibald MacLeish, and e.e cummings. He graduated with high honors in 1941 and married Cicely d'Autremont, a history student at Vassar. He briefly went to Harvard Law School, but never graduated. Instead he joined the U.S. Army, enrolling, along with his father, in the Office of Strategic Services (OSS), America's newly formed intelligence service. In 1943, he was stationed in London, assigned to X-2, the counterintelligence section of the OSS. Because X-2 had access to the product of Britain's intelligence interceptions, including its code-breaking, it operated under a tight regime of secrecy under which information was only available on a need-to-know basis. According to William Hood, who had served with Angleton in both the X-2 and the CIA, Angleton's experience in X-2 shaped his view of how counterintelligence should be handled.

When the OSS was dissolved in 1945, Angleton was assigned to a secret intelligence unit, called the "Central Intelligence Group," which became the CIA in 1947. Re-assigned to its Washington headquarters in 1949, he acted as the CIA liaison with the British, French, Italian, and West German intelligence services. In 1954, he was made the chief of the newly-created Counterintelligence Staff, a position which he held until Christmas Eve of 1975 when he retired from the CIA.

After his death, his actual achievements were eclipsed by his legend. In the media, he was transmogrified into the CIA's version of a Captain Ahab wreaking destruction of all around him by his pursuit of his own phantasmagorical great white whale. Books on the CIA depicted him as a paranoid mole hunter obsessively searching for non-existing spies planted in the heart of the CIA and non-existing deception plots aimed at the American government. His legend also became the stuff of fiction. He was the basis for a deranged and paranoid spy hunter in everything from movies, such as The Good Shepherd (where he is played by Matt Damon) and TV mini-series, such as The Company (where he is played by Michael Keaton) to novels, such as Norman Mailer's Harlot's Ghost. Like many legends, his portrayal had some basis in reality. It is true that he had deep-seated suspicions about KGB operations that could be construed as paranoia. It is also true that he conducted a 20 year long mole hunt that he believed both the CIA and FBI were vulnerable to Soviet penetration at the highest level, and that KGB passed disinformation through intelligence channels to the White House. Even though these contentions of a state-sponsored conspiracy to manipulate Presidents of the United States made him the object of ridicule in the media, the question remains: Was Angleton right?

Part One

DOWN THE RABBIT HOLE

1. Flowers of Deception

I first met James Jesus Angleton in February 1976. At that time, I knew nothing about his secret world of deception. Nor had I even heard of the concepts of "disinformation," "dangles," "false flags" or "penetrations," which were central elements in it.

I had just begun a book on Lee Harvey Oswald, the alleged assassin of President John F. Kennedy. Although Oswald had been investigated by the Warren Commission, the FBI, and other intelligence services, there was still a missing piece in the jigsaw puzzle -- the nearly two years that he had spent in the Soviet Union before he returned to the United States in 1962. What had happened to Oswald during this period? Had he had connections with Soviet intelligence during this Russian period? Had the KGB sponsored his return to the US? Had he been given any mission in America?

I had now been offered an opportunity to exclusively interview a man who supposedly could provide definitive answers to all these questions -- Yuri Nosenko. He was the KGB officer who had not only superintended Oswald's handling in Moscow in 1959 but had also reviewed his entire KGB file after the assassination. Nosenko then defected to the CIA. Not even the Warren Commission had been allowed to interview him. Now Donald Jamison, who was handling Nosenko on behalf of the CIA, had made him available for a book I was writing for the Reader's Digest Press. "Nosenko is utterly reliable on the subject of Oswald," Jamison had assured me, "He had full access to his KGB records." How could I refuse such an offer?

I had begun my interviews with Nosenko in January 1976. After I had completed six hours of interviews with Nosenko, I found several of the assertions he made about the KGB's treatment of Oswald inconsistent with other evidence furnished the Warren Commission. Even though I was assured by his CIA handler that he was utterly reliable on the subject, and had full access to KGB records, as he claimed, I was not completely satisfied. His insistence that the KGB had never contacted Oswald during his stay in the Soviet Union seemed implausible since Oswald had loudly advertised on his arrival there that he had some secret information of special interest to the Soviet Union.

My doubts were not entirely alleviated by Nosenko? I had lunch later that week in January with a Soviet diplomat in Washington, Igor Agou, to facilitate getting a visa to go to Russia. When I told Agou that I wanted to interview a number of Russian citizens who had been acquaintances of Oswald, he replied, "There is no need for you to go to Russia." Lowering his voice to a whisper, he added, "The best source on Oswald's visit there is in America. He is Yuri Nosenko." I found it curious that the Soviet Embassy would recommend that I see a Soviet traitor: the same traitor the CIA had recommended.

I went back to see Jamison. I asked him why, if Nosenko was such a valuable source, the Warren Commission had not called him as a witness in 1964. After all, the Commission noted in its report that it lacked access to the Soviet files on Oswald. According to both Jamison and Agou, Nosenko could have filled that gap.

He said there had been some "minor problem" with Nosenko at that time. They were "technicalities" about his defection that had now been cleared up. When I asked about the problem, he said that it was "too sensitive" to be discussed. He closed the issue by saying, "In any case, it is not relevant to your book. Don't worry about it further."

But I did. I began looking for an ex-CIA officer who would know about the problem with Nosenko in 1964. In 1975, the investigative reporter Seymour Hersh had published a story in the New York Times reporting an illegal CIA counterintelligence activity that resulted in the firing of a number of CIA executives. The most prominent was James Jesus Angleton. On checking his name, I found that he had also been a liaison with the Warren Commission.

Making contact with Angleton was not difficult; he was listed in the Virginia telephone directory. When told him on the phone that I had interviewed Nosenko, he said "I wouldn't have thought they would be letting him out so soon -- but I would be very interested in what he has to say." He agreed to meet me for dinner at the Madison Hotel, which he chose because it had a "secure garage."

He arrived in a black homburg, looking like someone that Central Casting might have chosen for the part of a counterintelligence chief. He was ghostly-thin, with deep-set eyes accentuated by arched eyebrows. He had an enigmatic smile, and a finely-sculptured face which, I later learned, had been proposed half-facetiously as a logo for the CIA.

He lit a cigarette and coughed as we sat down. He said he suffered from emphysema and ulcers. A quarter of a century in counterintelligence had evidently exacted some toll.

Since Angleton's counterintelligence staff had the responsibility for evaluating information supplied by KGB defectors, I assumed that he would be in a position to clarify what Nosenko had told me about Oswald and the KGB. I had no idea then that Nosenko had been the subject of a bitter ten-year battle inside the CIA that had destroyed a half-dozen careers. I merely wanted to know why the Warren Commission had not called Nosenko. I asked him, "Was there any problem with Nosenko's veracity?"

Angleton answered, with a thin smile, suggesting a deliberate understatement, "There are always problems when it comes to defectors." He explained that his job was establishing the bona fides of defectors. And that was not always possible.

"Did you award Nosenko his bona fides?" I asked.

He said he could not discuss individual cases, and moved on to another subject of which I had no understanding at all: orchids.

"There are over ten thousand identified species of orchids divided into tribes," I heard him say. He was describing orchid tribes, growing at different levels of a rain forest, with such exotic names as Dendrobian, Phalaenopsis, Cattleya, Cymbidian, and Brassia.

company him to an orchid supplier called Kens-
Maryland.

the following week. He talked as we walked
greenhouse as if he were conducting a lecture

What fascinated him about these orchids were their deceptive qualities. It has not been the fittest but the most deceptive orchid that has survived, he said. The perpetuation of most species of orchids depends on their ability to misrepresent themselves to insects. Having no food to offer the insects, they had to deceive them into landing on them and carrying their pollen to another orchid in their tribe. Orchids are too dispersed in nature to depend on the wind to carry their pollen.

To accomplish this deception, orchids use color, shape and odor to mimic something that attracts insects to their pods of pollen. Some orchids play on the sexual instincts of insects. The Trichoceros orchid, for example, so perfectly mimics in three dimensions the underside of a female fly, down to the hairs and smell, that it triggers mating response from passing male flies. Seeing what he thinks is a female fly, the male fly swoops down on the orchid, and attempts to have sex with it -- a process called pseudo-copulation. The motion causes the fly to hit the pollen pod, which attaches itself to his underside. The fly thus becomes an unwitting carrier. When it then passes another Trichoceros orchid, and repeats the frustrating process, it pollinates that orchid.

Other orchids play on the survival instinct of insects. Some Oncidium orchids have an almost exact replica of a bee's head on their petals. When a passing wasp sees this image of danger lurking behind it, a survival mechanism is triggered. The wasp plunges its stinger through its illusionary foe. The stinger passes through the petal into the pollen pod, which then adheres to it. When the wasp sees another Oncidium orchid, it provokes the same response, which pollinates the orchid. Angleton called this process of provocation "pseudo-attack".

In yet another twist on this theme, orchids lure insects to them by emitting odors that mimic those of nectar and other food sources. This lures the insect into the orchid's maze-like structure where instead of finding the nectar it runs into the pollen. This deception is especially effective against the mosquito which, while looking for nectar in a narrow tunnel, gets the pollen pod jammed into its eye. Unable to see, it flies away. When it smells similar nectar, it delivers the pollen. He said that such deceptions work because identifications in nature are often keyed to a single signal.

By this time, it had become clear that he was talking about how an intelligence service can be similarly duped, seduced, provoked, blinded, and lured down false trails. At a long leisurely lunch in Georgetown, I returned to the subject of Nosenko. Was Angleton suggesting that a KGB defector like Nosenko could have mimicked a real defector?

He answered "Soviet intelligence certainly has that capacity".

"The capacity to send out false defectors?"

"You know about The Trust"?

I shook my head, I had not heard of The Trust. "Is it connected to the Nosenko case?"

He answered, "If you want to understand Soviet deception, you have to go back to The Trust. Otherwise, you'll just waste my time. Talk to the Rock. He'll tell you all about it."

2. The Trust

The Rock was Raymond Rocca, a tall, bearded man in his early sixties, who looked more like a college professor than Angleton's chief of research at the CIA. Rocca had met Angleton in Italy in 1945 when they were in the OSS. When Angleton organized his counterintelligence staff, he gave Rocca the job of keeping track of what Angleton called "the serials:" bits of stray information from previous cases that might fit into other jigsaw puzzles. He remained at that job for the quarter of the century he spent in the ton was fired from the CIA in January 1975, Roc-

occa in February 1976, he was recovering from
eration. Since he was too weak to leave his home
in Falls Church, Virginia, I visited him there. He too collected orchids. Two giant Cattleya orchids flanked the door to his den, where we talked.

"The Trust," he explained, was a clandestine organization that operated in the Soviet Union from 1921 to 1928. Its official title was the Monarchist Union of Central Russia, and, as the name implied, its putative purpose was overthrowing the Communist regime in Russia and restoring a monarchy. Its headquarters was a municipal credit association in downtown Moscow, which provided a suitable cover for all its communications to its agents inside Russia. Because it operated out of a bank, it became known among anti-communist conspirators outside of Russia as "The Trust."

Anti-communist exiles in Europe first heard of the existence of this resistance organization in September 1921 from a Soviet official named Aleksandrovich Yakushev. On his way to an international lumber conference in Oslo, he slipped away from his delegation and contacted a leader of the anti-Communist movement in Estonia. He explained to him that though he was outwardly working for the Communists, he, and other high officials of the Soviet government, had come to the conclusion that Communism was infeasible in Russia. He also confided that they had formed a group, The Trust. He claimed that it had been so successful in recruiting government officials disillusioned with Communism that it was now the underground equivalent of a government-in-exile, with its members infiltrated in all key ministries, including the secret police. He then asked to be put in touch with other leaders of the anti-Soviet movement abroad, suggesting that The Trust would act as the "service organization" for them inside Russia. It would arrange through its network of collaborators to smuggle out whatever secret documents these exile groups needed.

Within a year, this offer was relayed to exile groups in Paris, Berlin, Vienna, and Helsinki -- and accepted. The exile groups outside of Russia received secret documents on the Soviet economy which they then passed on to Western intelligence services, which paid them handsomely for the information. This triangular trade in secrets -- from The Trust to the exiles to Western intelligence -- continued for six years. The Trust also furnished fake passports and visas for exiles to smuggle themselves, or their relatives, in or out of Russia. It also delivered arms and supplies to their partisans. It even contracted to undertake sabotage and assassination missions for them in Moscow and Petrograd. One by one, all the exiled leaders came to accept The Trust. So did the intelligence services of France, Germany, England, Austria, Sweden, and Finland.

Rocca then came to the point. The Trust only appeared to be an anti-Soviet organization. In reality, it was a creature of the Soviet secret police, designed to perfectly mimic a resistance organization. Its purpose was to manipulate real anti-Communist organizations into misleading the West.

"What of Yakushev?" I asked.

Rocca explained that he was a "dangle." A dangle is someone who feigns disaffection from his government and, like bait, is put in the path of opposition intelligence services. Yakushev, under the control of the secret police, was able to offer precisely the kinds of help -- especially in saving relatives -- that the exiles were most likely to be enticed by into the trap. Since the secret police were running the show, he could guarantee the success of the smuggling and assassinations. The Trust also staged sufficient dramatic encounters, such as car chases and gun fights, to lend a convincing air of reality to the masquerade. (It even arranged tours of the "underground" for émigré writers through carefully staged "Potemkin villages.")

The deception succeeded in neutralizing most of the anti-Communist exile groups and luring back into the Soviet Union leading anti-Communists, such as Sydney Reilly and Boris Savinkov, who were arrested, given show trials and executed. As an added bonus, it earned enough money from the sale of secrets to eleven Western intelligence services to finance all the activities of Soviet intelligence for a decade.

"Wasn't the loss of this information damaging to the Soviet Union?"

Rocca replied that it was "disinformation" a term coined by the German General Staff in the First World War. It can be either factually accurate information or fake information, or a concoction of both. The important part is its aim. According to the KGB manual "Disinformation, it is directed at misleading the enemy concerning questions of state policy."

In the case of The Trust, Soviet intelligence (called the OGPU) received orders from Lenin himself to give Western intelligence services a picture of Soviet economic weakness so dire that Western intervention in the Soviet Union was unnecessary. By making it appear that this information was stolen by dissidents, Soviet intelligence made it much more credible.

When the deception began to wear thin in 1929, Soviet intelligence ordered the head of The Trust, Edward Opperput, to himself "defect" to the West in Finland. Opperput confessed to Finnish interrogators that The Trust was a sham organization from the start. His revelations had the intended effect of demoralizing the exiles and sowing confusion among the Western intelligence services that had depended on the Trust for information about Russia. Once this final coup was accomplished, Opperput re-defected to Russia, and returned to his duties in the Soviet secret service.

Rocca explained that in the intelligence business defectors were defined as either "bona fide" or "dispatched" depending on who controlled their actions. If a defector only pretended to change sides, he was "dispatched."

I asked, "Was Nosenko thought to be a dispatched defector?"

"He could have been dispatched," Rocca answered. "His message to the CIA about Oswald could have been disinformation cooked up by the KGB."

"But was there any evidence that he was dispatched?"

Rocca lit his pipe and said, "You're talking about operational data. I was never involved in that. I thought you just wanted a historical perspective." It was clear that the seminar on The Trust was over.

As he walked me to the door, I asked if he could recommend someone familiar with the "operational data" of the Nosenko case.

He replied, as if he had been waiting for the question, "The man you want to see is Scotty Miler." I realized that Angleton had arranged a series of guides into his universe of deception.

3. The Desert

Newton "Scotty" Miler, after leaving the CIA in 1975, had moved to Cuba, New Mexico. When I arrived, he had just returned from hunting rabbits in the desert. He was a powerfully-built man, with a boyish face, wearing a denim jacket that made him look like a cowboy. He made no effort to conceal his bitterness towards the CIA, telling me he had moved to the desert "to get as far away from the CIA as possible." He had joined the CIA in 1950, and, like Rocca, had spent almost his entire career working with Angleton. As Angleton's chief of operations, he had analyzed the Nosenko case for nearly ten years.

He picked up the thread exactly where Rocca had left it. He began by saying matter-of-factly, "Nosenko was a dispatched KGB agent. That is why he never got his bona fides. That is also why the Warren Commission could not use him as a witness."

Now my question was answered. And I told Scotty I would be returning that evening to DC.

As he walked me to car, he said, "There was another problem we were unable to settle in the Nosenko case: the KGB would not risk dispatching Nosenko if they did not have someone already inside the CIA."

"Are you saying that the KGB had a mole in the CIA in 1964?"

"That is what this case was always about -- and is still about."

When I called Angleton from my motel room that night, he told me he could not speak on the phone. He suggested I meet him at his home in Tucson, Arizona.

I was surprised to find that Angleton lived in what amounted to a huge private park in downtown Tucson. From the porch of his ranch house, one couldn't see another house or a sign of the city. He proudly showed me furniture that he had designed and built himself. He evidently enjoyed designing his own world.

We sat on his terrace. Looking into the darkness, he told me that if I had arrived earlier while it was still light, I could have seen the mountains. He then proceeded to sketch out for me with his finger, peak by peak, the view I might have seen.

There were many fireflies blinking in the distance. Calling my attention to them, he said that the female firefly used a sort of Morse code of flashes to signal males of her availability. "But of course one can't be sure it's a female firefly," he explained, because the Photuris Versicolor beetle, the firefly's predator, duplicated the flashes to lure the male firefly into a trap.

When we returned to the subject of Nosenko, Angleton told me that the case remained unsolved when he left the CIA. Since the counterintelligence files painstakingly compiled for 20 years had been largely destroyed by now, and the institutional memory of the CIA "wiped clean," he doubted it could ever be re-opened. He said that the theory his counterintelligence staff had been working on was that Nosenko was the "outside man" sent in by the KGB to divert attention away from an "inside man," or mole.

I told him I planned to interview Nosenko the next week.

"You never will be allowed to see him again," he answered. And as I learned the following week through Jamison, he was right. Nosenko had decided to terminate the interview.

Fascinated by his concept of deception, I continued to see Angleton on my trips to Washington. One of our lunches at the Madison Hotel lasted so long that, when the waiters began setting up for dinner, Angleton suggested we stay for dinner. It was the longest meal I have ever had. Late into the dinner hour, as he meticulously peeled away the layers of an onion, he described a picture in a book of Gestalt psychology experiments that illustrated what he considered to be the "mind of the state" problem. The image could be seen two ways: As the profiles of two heads or as a wine cup. He said that if one expected to see the double heads, they popped into focus. If one expected to see the wine cup, one saw it, not two heads. But one could not see both pictures at the same time. His point was meant to apply to the interpretation of intelligence. The same data, like the picture, could be seen either as an intelligence coup or a deception operation: which was Nosenko?

4. The Incubus

I next went to see Richard M. Helms in Tehran. Before becoming the US Ambassador to Iran, he had been CIA Director. I had been introduced to Helms three years earlier by an Iranian lawyer. At that time, Helms, always blunt, ask that I not ask him about either the CIA or the Kennedy assassination.

Now I needed to ask him the subjects he had embargoed. To my surprise he invited me to stay at the embassy. I told him soon after my arrival that I had interviewed Nosenko.

Helms replied in an angry tone that the CIA "had no business giving you Nosenko in this way." He told me that Nosenko had been given a carefully-rehearsed brief by the CIA to pass on to me. And, by doing so, it had re-opened old wounds.

"Angleton's wounds?" I asked.

"It goes much deeper, I am afraid," he said. He explained that in 1964, when Nosenko defected, "Nosenko's reliability was key to determining what the KGB had to do with Oswald." Attorney General Robert F. Kennedy and Chief Justice Earl Warren wanted to call him as a witness in the investigation. So Helms went to see the

Chief Justice in his chambers, insisting no notes be taken. He told Warren there were "two schools of thought on Nosenko" within the CIA. The first held that he was a legitimate defector and could be believed about Oswald. The second held that he was still a KGB plant sent to misinform the US. He then advised the Chief Justice not to see Nosenko until the matter was resolved. Chief Justice Warren agreed and Nosenko was never called as a witness.

"Was the situation later resolved," I asked.

Helms replied, "Never to my satisfaction. It still hangs like an incubus over the CIA." He told me the reason he had agreed to see me. A month before, he had a visit from a CIA officer named John Hart who said he was re-investigating the matter. "What I'm going to tell you is exactly what I told Hart. I have no memory of the details of the case."

"But who does," I asked.

He jotted down a number of names on piece of paper. At the top of the list was Tennent Bagley, Jr.

Helms told me Pete Bagley, as he was called, came from a prominent tobacco family in North Carolina. Both his brothers had become fleet admirals in the U.S. Navy. His cousin had served as a Presidential press secretary. Bagley wanted to be head of the CIA. At the age of 25, after getting a PhD in political science at the University of Geneva, he went to work for the CIA. In 1950, he became a case officer in the key Soviet Russia Division, which recruited Soviet sources. He became its deputy director in 1962, which was when he met Nosenko. He ran him as a spy for 2 years and then, after the Kennedy assassination, arranged his defection to the United States. "He knows more than anyone else about the Nosenko case," Helms said, "Last I heard he lives in Brussels. Go see him."

I asked whether I could tell him about our conversation.

Helms thought for a moment while he poured himself a poire brandy. Then answered, "Yes, and tell him you have a message from me: this guy John Hart is after his scalp."

5. Bagley's Story

When I arrived at my hotel in Brussels, I found a note from Bagley telling me to meet him the next day at the Waterloo battlefield, which was about a half hour from Brussels. He said at precisely noon he would be standing in front of the circular mural of the great battle in the museum.

I had no trouble recognizing him. He looked considerably younger than his fifty years. He then suggested that he take me for a tour of the battlefield. He guided me from position to position, explaining the vulnerability of Napoleon's position, with the same kind of authority with which in the weeks to come he would guide me through the Nosenko case.

This latter tour required delving into the inner sanctum of the CIA's deception operations. Over dinner at the Villa Lorraine, a three-star restaurant outside Brussels, he said in a hushed tone, "You should know what you are getting into. Nosenko was not just another case -- it was at the heart of everything that happened at the CIA for a decade."

Bagley's story differed from Angleton's in one important respect. Angleton had omitted telling me that Nosenko had been working for the CIA for two years before the assassination of Kennedy. "He was our man in Moscow," Bagley said, "I should know. I recruited him."

This missing piece meant that Nosenko, who claimed to be Oswald's case officer in Russia, could have been reporting to the CIA about Oswald before the assassination. Bagley deferred answering that question. He said I first needed to understand "the context." That took nearly 6 weeks of meetings in a house I rented in Gassin, a mountain town above St. Tropez in France.

Bagley began his story in Switzerland in 1962. At the time, officially, he was the Second Secretary at the US Embassy in Berne; unofficially, he was working for the CIA's elite Soviet Russia Division, code-named BK HERALD. His job was recruiting Russian diplomats, military attaches, intelligence officers or other government officials who were traveling through or temporarily stationed in the West. They were called REDTOPS. When he found a promising REDTOP, Bagley arranged for him to be approached by an "access agent," who could be someone outside the CIA with a plausible excuse to approach the target. In one case, the access agent was a back doctor. Bagley then would attempt to induce the REDTOP to steal secrets for the CIA. Often that meant compromising the RED-TOP. It was not an easy job particularly since many of the candidates were "dangles," sent out by the KGB to test CIA procedures.

On June 8th, 1962, Bagley got an urgent call from an American diplomat in Geneva. A Russian security officer named Yuri Ivanovich Nosenko had passed him a note at the Disarmament Conference. It said he wanted to be put in touch with a representative of the U.S. Government.

Bagley caught the next plane to Geneva. Working through the American diplomat, he passed a message back to Nosenko containing only a time and an address. The address was that of a "safe house" that the CIA maintained in Geneva for just such a contingency. It was a small apartment with a terrace in an inconspicuous building that would be used only once, for Nosenko, and then abandoned in case Nosenko turned out to be a KGB "dangle."

As he waited for Nosenko to show up, Bagley was joined in the apartment by George Kisvalter. Kisvalter, a CIA specialist in the Soviet Union, was born in Russia and spoke perfect Russian. He had been sent that afternoon from Washington to assist Bagley with the interrogation.

Nosenko arrived an hour and a half late, claiming he had to make sure he wasn't followed. He was a powerfully built man, about six feet tall, with a massive jaw. He acted as if he knew the drill. He also said that he knew that the CIA was secretly taping the session. Even so, he rattled off answers to the questions as if he was there for a job interview.

The first question was mandated by CIA regulations for all RED-TOPS. Kisvalter asked Nosenko whether he knew of any imminent

Soviet plans to launch a military attack.

Nosenko smiled, as if he was expecting the question, and then shook his head no.

He was next asked why he had contacted the CIA. A CIA Directive on Defectors warned that some were dispatched by the KGB to "convey false or deceptive information to U.S. Intelligence services."

Nosenko replied that his motive was money. He said he had spent 900 Swiss francs of KGB funds on a drinking binge and needed to replace it. In return, he offered to furnish the CIA with a KGB manual on its surveillance techniques in Moscow. He said it would explain how the KGB had caught one of the CIA's top agents in Moscow.

Bagley asked Nosenko if he wanted to defect to the West.

Nosenko answered "No." He said that he had no intention of defecting. He had a wife and children in Moscow.

This was the answer Bagley hoped to hear. The object of the exercise was not to encourage REDTOPS to defect but to get them to stay in their jobs and spy for the CIA. He gave Nosenko the 900 francs. He told him the CIA would pay him handsomely if he assisted in the future. He offered $25,000 for each Soviet source in the West his information helped expose. The money would be deposited in a Swiss account.

Nosenko betrayed no emotional reaction at this offer to commit treason. He shrugged and said he would consider it.

Bagley still didn't know with whom he was dealing. In response to his "flash" cable, CIA files had no "traces" on Yuri Nosenko. The only Nosenko that turned up was Ivan Nosenko, the Soviet Minister of Shipbuilding, and a member of the Central Committee of the Communist Party, who had died six years earlier.

Nosenko told Bagley he was Ivan Nosenko's son. He supplied

a brief biography, saying he had been born October 20, 1927 in Nikolayev, Russia and had attended the elite Frunze Military Academy. In 1953, after serving in naval intelligence, he had joined the KGB. He was then assigned to its Second Chief Directorate, which had the primary responsibility for recruiting foreigners in Russia. Nosenko now worked through the Directorate's "American Department" to recruit U.S. embassy employees in Moscow, and its "Tourist Department" to recruit American tourists in Russia.

"If so, what was he doing in Geneva," Bagley asked.

Nosenko said he had been given this trip abroad as a perk.

Bagley realized that, if his story checked out, Nosenko was an incredible catch. Not only was he the son of a hero of the Soviet Union -- Khrushchev himself had been a guard of honor at Ivan Nosenko's funeral -- but he was in the 2nd Chief Directorate, which, up until 1959, the CIA did not know existed. No one had ever been recruited from this Directorate before. If Nosenko could be induced to go back to Moscow and work as an agent in place, the CIA would have a mole in the heart of KGB counterintelligence.

"It seemed almost too good to be true," Bagley recalled. As the Geneva debriefing proceeded, Nosenko provided a wealth of clues to identify Soviet agents in the United States and England. He also revealed how the KGB had planted microphones in the U.S. Embassy in Moscow. The interview lasted two hours.

Two days later, he returned for another session. He brought the promised documents on surveillance. They revealed that the KGB been spraying a chemical substance on the shoes of American diplomats in Moscow, so that they could be followed by surveillance teams.

"Will you work for us in Moscow?" Asked Bagley.

"Yes," he answered, but only on condition that the CIA made no attempt to contact him there. He explained it would be "too dangerous."

On June 11th, Bagley cabled the CIA in Washington: "Subject has conclusively proved his bona fides. He has provided info of importance and sensitivity. Willing to meet when abroad." The CIA gave Nosenko the cryptonym AE FOXTROT and authorized Bagley to provide him with a secret writing kit, a password, and a means of communicating with the CIA. Four days later Nosenko returned to Moscow.

Bagley then flew to Washington where he was personally commended by David Murphy, the Chief of the Soviet Russia Division. Murphy told him that he had "hooked the biggest fish yet." The next step is what the CIA called "career management" through which Nosenko's career in the KGB would be systematically advanced by the CIA. This feat involved arranging for a mole to have a string of dramatic successes in his intelligence work, even if it meant sacrificing pawns to advance him. The goal was to burrow the mole Nosenko deeper into the KGB's command structure.

Before any moves in this game were made, Bagley was abruptly summoned to see Angleton. Angleton had no direct authority over him, and Bagley usually resented his interference, but the Nosenko case proved different. Angleton handed him a file to read about another REDTOP defector, saying, "Read this before you proceed with FOXTROT."

As Bagley read it that weekend, he saw that the Nosenko case had a sinister dimension. Each bit of information Nosenko had provided exactly mirrored information already given by this earlier defector. Angleton's concern was that Nosenko had been sent by the KGB to Geneva to supply data to divert the CIA away from the leads supplied by the earlier defector. The practice was called in the CIA "painting false tracks." Had he been duped by Nosenko?

Angleton told Bagley that now that the CIA knew it was dealing with a KGB "controlled source," Nosenko could be turned to the CIA's advantage, using him as a "mailbox" in which it would deposit disinformation messages for the KGB.

What about information Nosenko provides, asked Bagley.

"No problem, pay him, and label his information as from a source whose bona fides have not been established."

Bagley returned to Switzerland crestfallen. The mole he had recruited turned out to be a Soviet plant. Now he had to wait for his return in this game of disinformation. But for 18 months there was no further word from AE FOXTROT.

The game changed for Bagley when President Kennedy was assassinated on November 22nd 1963. The CIA established that the alleged assassin, Lee Harvey Oswald, had attempted to contact Soviet intelligence in Moscow during his stay there. And if Oswald had made contact with the KGB, his case would have been handled by the 2nd Chief Directorate's "Tourist Department." That was precisely where Bagley's AE FOXTROT was located. Since Bagley believed that he had been dispatched to the CIA by the KGB, he realized, as he put it, he was "sitting on a time bomb."

Some six weeks later, Nosenko sent a cable to an innocuous-sounding address in Europe. It was the pre-arranged signal that Nosenko had been given by the CIA. He indicated he would be arriving in Geneva the following week, where he would again be acting as the security officer for the Soviet disarmament delegation. He wanted a meeting with "George," the name by which he knew Bagley.

Bagley was in Washington, where he now headed his Soviet Russia Division's counterintelligence operations (which had no connection with Angleton's counterintelligence Staff.) As soon as Nosenko's signal was flashed to Washington, Bagley booked a flight to Geneva. He expected merely another meeting. On January 23rd, 1964, Nosenko sauntered into the CIA's safe house, taking few precautions about security. He greeted Bagley like an old friend. As he poured himself a drink, he casually told Bagley he had made a "decision." Instead of returning to Russia, he would defect to the United States.

Even if he believed Nosenko was genuine, CIA policy was to discourage defections, and persuade REDTOPS to return to the Soviet Union, where they could do some good as spies. Since he believed

Nosenko was phony, and controlled by the KGB, such a defection would be ludicrous. But before Bagley turned down this defection, Nosenko had another surprise. He said with an ugly smile "Are your tape recorders running?"

Bagley did not answer.

Nosenko then announced that he had information about Lee Harvey Oswald that could be crucially important to the United States. Nosenko explained that he had been the KGB officer assigned to Oswald's case when he arrived in Moscow. He was kept in the loop after he returned to the United States in 1962. Then, after the assassination in 1963, he had been asked to read through Oswald's entire KGB file and "sign off" on the case for the KGB. This put him in a unique position: he could testify to the entire relationship between Oswald and the KGB.

Bagley was totally unprepared for this turn of events. Even though he didn't believe Nosenko, he knew that Nosenko's claim he was Oswald's case officer would set off bells in the CIA. The President might have to be briefed on the case. There was nothing he could do but continue the interrogation session.

He asked the key question. "What interest did the KGB have in Oswald?"

"It was decided Oswald was of no interest whatsoever, so the KGB recommended he go home to the United States," Nosenko answered.

Bagley now suspected that Nosenko's job was to clear the KGB. Changing the subject, he asked him why he now wanted to defect.

Nosenko had a pat answer. He said that he had come under suspicion and feared he would be arrested if he returned to Russia. He said he had just received a telegram ordering him to return to Moscow on February 4th. He had less than a week. He needed help from the CIA.

When the transcript of this interrogation was cabled to CIA headquarters, Helms had no choice but to authorize a "crash" defection for Nosenko. If he had done otherwise, the CIA could be accused of suppressing potentially important evidence on the Kennedy assassination. He gave Bagley the "Go" signal. He specified Nosenko was to be taken out of Switzerland "black," or without revealing his identity to the Swiss. A military attaché plane, not opened to border inspection, would be used.

After a brief stop at the U.S. debriefing center in Frankfurt, Nosenko arrived in Washington on a military transport on February 11 1964 and was put in a CIA safe house outside of Washington.

The issue was what to do with him. Bagley's investigators, after scrutinizing his biography, concluded it was a "legend", concocted by the KGB since Nosenko could not have held the positions he claimed to have had in the KGB. They concluded that Nosenko was a dispatched defector under KGB control. Bagley concurred, as did his Chief, David Murphy.

Murphy feared that the KGB might have instructed Nosenko to break away at his earliest opportunity and go to a Soviet Embassy. He could then denounce the CIA for attempting to kidnap him. He might even claim the CIA was attempting to suppress his Oswald story. On February 17, less than a week after Nosenko's arrival, Murphy wrote Helms: "There is greater evidence now I believe for the view that this operation is designed for long-term goals of utmost importance to the Soviets. One of these is probably a massive propaganda assault on the CIA in which subject, most probably as a 're-defected CIA agent,' will play a major role." In addition, he expressed concern that Nosenko's mission also included the "penetration of our operational effort," which could be accomplished by Nosenko learning CIA procedures, and the "protection of past or possibly existing sources," which he could do by confusing ongoing investigations with false clues. Because of all the damage Nosenko could do, Murphy recommended that preparations be made to imprison Nosenko, if only to prevent him from re-defecting. He noted "the big problem is one of timing: how long can we keep subject or his KGB controllers, ignorant of our awareness of this operation?" At some point, he would have to be confronted and broken through hostile interrogation.

Bagley knew that this measure was strongly opposed by Angleton. Angleton argued that Nosenko, and his KGB controllers, should be played "like a fish on a line." He did not even want Nosenko to be told he failed all his polygraph tests. But Murphy wanted more immediate results. He believed he would break under pressure. As Nosenko had involved himself in the investigation of Oswald, Helms, over the objections of Angleton, authorized the hostile interrogation.

To lull Nosenko's suspicions, the CIA paid him $60,000 for the information he supplied, began making arrangements for him to be a U.S. citizen and even sent him on a vacation to Hawaii with Bagley. All the while he was on the beach; the CIA was constructing a vault-like prison for him in the basement of a ranch house outside Washington.

Then, on April 4th 1964, Nosenko was again strapped into a lie detector in a carefully rehearsed drama designed to break him. His interrogators told him that his answers were lies. He asked for Bagley. Bagley came in, examined the lie detector results, and ordered him stripped and put in a windowless cell.

Nosenko spent the next three and a half years in solitary confinement. Day and night, the light remained on in his eight foot square cell, with guards keeping him under constant observation. Every three or four days, he was brought in front of interrogators, and grilled relentlessly about details of his story. As the weeks dragged on without results, they tried various disorientation techniques, such as gradually setting clocks back and manipulating lighting conditions to convince him it was day when it was really night, confusing his sense of time. At one point, Bagley was convinced that he was about to break, and admit his entire biography was a KGB invention. He muttered something indicating that he could not have held the positions in the KGB he had claimed to hold. Bagley held his breathe, anticipating that a full confession would follow. When it didn't, he repeated the question. After a long pause, Nosenko replied "You misunderstood me." He then pulled himself together, and stuck monotonously to his story.

The battle went on year after year. It was Bagley versus Nosenko.

Bagley set forth the case against Nosenko in a 900-page report. "But he never broke," Bagley said, as he ended his story.

Then Nosenko was released, given $160,000 by the CIA, and made a counterintelligence consultant for the CIA. Bagley did not know what had happened to transform him in the eyes of the CIA from a provocateur on a KGB mission to an accredited defector.

Bagley also had a reversal of fortune. In late 1967, his Soviet Russia Division was "re-staffed." David Murphy, the division head, was sent to Paris to be station chief there, and Bagley was transferred to Belgium. His Washington career clearly ended, he applied for early retirement. Then he found out that every top CIA officers who had been involved in the Nosenko was sent to a foreign assignment. The entire case seemed to him to be turned inside out. The insiders who had developed the indictment against Nosenko were out. Nosenko, who had been the Division responsibility, was suddenly turned over to the CIA's Office of Security.

Bagley said to me with biting irony "the KGB agent gets a $160,000 pay day for duping the Agency while the CIA officers who had exposed him are given early retirement."

(Nosenko was still on the CIA payroll when he died at the age of 81 on August 23, 2008.)

When I raised the subject of John Hart, he told me he had paid him a visit three months earlier in Brussels. Recalling Helm's warning, I asked him, "why is John Hart after your scalp?"

"Hart's job is to rewrite history," he replied. "That is what the CIA does best. Ask Angleton."

I took Bagley's advice, and went again to see Angleton. He told me that the wounds inflicted by the Nosenko mission were not, however, so easily healed. His immediate concern was how the KGB seemed to learn about developments in the case even though it was one of the closest held secrets in the CIA. He had his counterintelligence staff test the idea that the KGB had possible feedback from a source inside the CIA's Soviet Russia Division by playing a "marked card." The "card" was false information about a planned operation against a KGB associate of Nosenko's stationed in Europe. It was provided only to CIA officers in the Soviet Russia Division with access to the Nosenko case. Somehow this bogus information resulted in the KGB officer's abrupt transfer back to Russia. As Angleton saw it, the marked card he played in the CIA had made its way back to the KGB in Moscow. If so, someone in the Soviet Russia Division was a KGB source. But who? Investigations were launched against seven CIA officers in the Division, including David Murphy and Bagley. None panned out, although, in the process, careers may have been ruined. Unable to find the leak, Angleton persuaded Helms to remove the entire Soviet Russia Division from sensitive cases. When he tried to extend the investigation to the FBI, which was also privy to the Nosenko case, an infuriated J. Edgar Hoover responded by severing the FBI's liaison with the CIA.

But why? Was Nosenko so important?

"Nosenko was never the real issue," Angleton told me. "What Bagley refused to see is that Nosenko is neither good nor evil. He is merely a messenger in an age-old game." It was a game of nations, international deception. It was his universe. And over the course of the next few weeks, he outlined for me the strange features of this universe.

Part Two

UNIVERSE OF DECEPTION

6. The Espionage Business

"Think of an espionage service as a highly specialized employment Service," said Angleton, over one of the longest lunches I ever had. It was at Harvey's, one of his favorite restaurants in Washington. "Intelligence officers are head hunters. They look for the recruits among foreign government officials with legitimate access to secret documents." They act much like conventional corporate headhunters, consulting biographical files to find a candidate to fill an opening, observe their work product or interviewing them, and then make them a tempting offer to change their loyalties. But unlike their counterparts in the private sector, these recruiters do not ask the candidate to give up his old jobs. Instead, they insist he maintain two positions simultaneously: one for his own government and one for his new and secret employer. They also provide a further service: promoting their career by providing them with "successes" in the form of information.

What the human espionage business is all about is the surreptitious theft of enemy secrets, or what is called in the CIA "collection." The whole idea is to get unexpected intelligence, or data that the enemy does not know is missing. Here the surreptitious part of the equation is crucial. Once an enemy finds out that one of its secrets is known, it can remedy or even take advantage of the theft. For example, once it knows that a code has been broken, it can use it to transmit messages it wants its adversaries to read.

The CIA is engaged in this business in the Soviet Russia and the KGB is engaged in it in the United States. Both sides attempt to find people in the heart of the enemy camp willing to steal and copy secrets.

It is generally a slow process in which bits of information are gradually fitted into a jigsaw puzzle. British intelligence, for example, obtained through espionage in the early 1930s the manuals and settings for encryption machines that were than being tested by the German Army. As long as the Germans were using secure land lines for communication, this intelligence had no practical value. Then the war required wireless transmissions. In the 1940s, after French and Polish intelligence stole a German cipher machine and British mathematicians built a machine to decipher these messages, the British were able to break these codes.

During this process, espionage services have a double job. First, they must steal secrets of value. Second, they must erase all traces of the theft and dupe their enemy into believing they are still secret.

The agent who does the actual theft is almost always an enemy national, since he must have access to classified secrets. So the CIA uses Russian intelligence officers, diplomats, military men, or other government officials. The KGB uses Americans willing to betray secrets.

At the CIA, the unit responsible for finding applicants for this work in the Soviet Union is the Soviet Russia Division. The targets are drawn mainly from the 10,000 to 15,000 Communist officials stationed in foreign countries. Like any other head hunting firm, the CIA maintains extensive biographic files, including clandestinely taken photographs, on them and their families.

At the KGB, the mirror image of the CIA's Soviet Russia Division is the American Department of its First Chief Directorate. Its case officers, when attached to Soviet embassies or missions and given diplomatic immunity, are called "legal residents." (When they operate otherwise, they are called "illegals.") According to KGB objectives intercepted in 1962, the highest priority is placed on obtaining agents who can supply codes and other cryptographic material that would allow it to intercept and read American military and other governmental messages.

When agents are recruited, espionage services then manage their careers so they can steal useful data. As a CIA directive notes, "we are prepared to guide and assist him in his career [in the Russian government], running him in place until he develops the access we need." To accomplish this feat, they provide agents with a means of safely communicating.

This trade craft was as old as the intelligence business itself, and Angleton learned it during his service in the OSS. But was the CIA vulnerable? The answer became apparent through his liaison with one of the most infamous Russian spies in history, Kim Philby.

7. Kim and Jim

Angleton met Philby on a rainy day in October 1949 at Harvey's Seafood House in downtown Washington, only a few blocks from his office at the CIA. He had fleetingly known Philby during his OSS training in London during World War II. The CIA brief he received in preparation for the lunch called him Britain's "top expert on Russian intelligence." It also provided a brief biography, noting:

Harold Adrian Russell Philby had been born on New Year's Day, 1912, in Ambala, India. His father, Harry St. John Philby, a British administrator in India, called him Kim after the character in the book by Rudyard Kipling. Philby went to school at Westminster in London, where, following in his father's footsteps, he was Captain of the School. He went on to Trinity College at Cambridge, which he graduated from with honors in 1933. He worked as a special correspondent for the Times in Spain during its civil war. In 1940, he reported on the British expeditionary force in France. His intelligence career began in February 1941, when he joined MI-6, the British espionage service. By 1942, he headed its counterintelligence in Spain and Portugal. He was commended for his success exposing German ruses and double-agents in the Iberian peninsula, then, in 1945, transferred to MI-6's "Section IX," which operated against the Soviet Union (even though it was an ally.) By the time the Cold War had begun he was in charge of its counterintelligence staff. His job was to entrap Russian intelligence officers in Europe and Turkey. His success in recruiting them led to his appointment as chief of MI6's anti-Soviet operations.

He had now come to Washington, according to the CIA brief, to coordinate Britain's anti-Soviet activities in Europe with those of the CIA, FBI, and Royal Canadian Mounted Police.

Angleton had himself only recently returned to Washington from a long intelligence service in Europe. In May 1949, he had been appointed to be the CIA's liaison with other allied intelligence services. This was a pivotal job since the CIA, which at the time was barely two years old, relied heavily on the British, French, Germans, and other allied services to do much of the recruitments and dirty work in post-war Europe. Since these "partners" were exempt from Congressional scrutiny, they provided one of the principal mechanisms through which the CIA organized the secret war against Soviet Russia in these early years. As head of this liaison, Angleton had immense power. This also entailed working closely with his counterpart in MI-6, Philby.

Angleton had much in common with his luncheon partner. They had been educated in England, spent much of their life abroad, and had similar literary and epicurean tastes. They liked English poetry, French wine, German music, and discussing Cabbages and Kings. They both shared an interest in a field that few outsiders knew existed: anti-Soviet operations.

Angleton knew from his briefing that Philby's assignment to Washington was anything but routine. Philby was not just another British intelligence executive furloughed to America; he was, as MI-6 had informed the CIA, next in line to head the British secret service. His mission was temporary but critical. It concerned what was to be the major, though secret, America initiative of that era.

After the successful Communist coup in Czechoslovakia in 1948, the United States government, with bipartisan support in Congress, had committed itself to rolling back Soviet influence in Eastern Europe. Yet U.S. leaders wanted to achieve this strategic objective by means short of war, which meant covert action. The mechanism for undertaking this secret offensive was the so called "Office of Planning Coordination," which was the CIA's paramilitary arm, staffed by former OSS subversion experts, and headed by Frank Wisner. It was charged with developing anti-Communist undergrounds in Communist countries in Eastern Europe. They would have their own guerrilla forces, saboteurs, and political front groups which would be used to disrupt communications, foment strikes, and paralyze economies. The ultimate goal was to undermine Soviet control.

Britain, with its half-century experience in East European espionage and its control over émigré groups in exile, had a major role in this ambitious undertaking. MI-6 would furnish what agents and other intelligence assets it had still operating in Eastern Europe and help coordinate their activities with those of the CIA. In this enterprise, Philby would work, through the Angleton liaison, directly with the CIA.

The centerpiece of the offensive was the underground in Poland, which was called WIN, the Polish acronym for "Freedom and Independence." Earlier that year, its representatives had made contact with Polish émigrés in London, and claimed that it had wide support in Poland and could now mobilize 30,000 guerrilla fighters. It had become, in this respect, the successor to the Polish Home Army that had fought the Germans to a standstill in 1944.

Although Wisner's Office of Policy Coordination was at first skeptical of these claims, WIN gradually provided concrete evidence of its ability to undertake guerrilla actions. It attacked police stations, blew up military installations, and even fought pitched battles against Soviet tanks -- the aftermaths of which were documented by photographs. Wisner insisted that all WIN needed was anti-tank weapons "to drive the Red Army out of Warsaw." Then WIN began smuggling out of Poland reports and documents revealing the Soviet order of battle and its military capabilities in Eastern Europe. This intelligence apparently came from WIN moles inside the Defense Ministry.

By the time Philby had arrived in Washington, the CIA's "Office of Policy Coordination" had begun parachuting arms and gold coins into Poland for WIN. It was also pressing British intelligence to get the Polish Government in Exile in London to fully support WIN as its inside arm in Poland, and have it put all its agents in direct contact with its operatives. Other dissident movements in the Ukraine, Georgia, Lithuania, Albania, and Hungary would be used to divert and distract Soviet attention from the main target: Poland. That was, at least, the plan at the time of the lunch at Harvey's.

Philby, after gossiping briefly about their old colleagues in London and his rough crossing of the Atlantic on the S.S. Caronia the week before, began complaining about his first order of business. He called it "Vetting the old Nazis." He explained that he had been given, among his other duties, the dirty job of checking through the files, and locating, the group of German counterintelligence officers who had been secretly re-located in Canada.

These Germans were of great importance to the planned offensive in Eastern Europe because they had the only available pool of potential agents. These were Polish and other Eastern European citizens who had been secretly turned into informers during the German occupation. Many had betrayed their comrades in the resistance to save their own lives, and, under German aegis, elevated themselves in the Communist underground. Some had been exposed, and were presumably dead or in prison, but others, who had managed to conceal their deadly secret, had gone on to work for the Communist regimes in their countries. Since they now could be possibly coerced into cooperating -- or else face the consequences of exposure -- they could be re-activated as agents (so long as the Soviets did not also find out.) These "assets" could then be employed to help WIN and other undergrounds stage an effective uprising. Philby needed to connect with the Royal Mounted Police, with whom Angleton worked closely, to get the records of the cadre of Hitler's ex-intelligence officers in Canada.

Over the next eighteen months, Angleton continued to lunch with Philby on a weekly basis. Usually they went to Harvey's or the Army and Navy Club. Meanwhile Philby had been appointed as the British representative to the "Special Policy Committee," which assessed the covert action offensive in East Europe. In this context, he steered the conversation to its intelligence problems, often lacing his assessments with waspish humor about naive Americans and his cynical view of world politics. He also presented a list of questions about CIA activities that he said had been drawn up by MI-6 in London. Of course, as CIA liaison, Angleton's job was to give him answers (unless the information was specifically embargoed.)

Meanwhile, the CIA was building up the capacity of WIN to

challenge Soviet power. The ex-German counterintelligence officers, many of whom had been vetted by Philby, provided a long list of their candidates with hidden pasts in Poland, and many of them were duly recruited by the CIA and put in contact with WIN. The CIA also furnished WIN with clandestine radios for WIN to transmit messages back to the CIA and sophisticated explosives and timers for sabotage.

Since the reports it received back from Poland suggested that WIN controlled entire regions, the CIA marshaled virtually the entire Polish émigré movement abroad to support the WIN "home army." By this time, it was receiving raw intelligence from WIN suggesting that Stalin was in such grave trouble in Russia that he was on the verge of losing control over Eastern Europe.

In the spring of 1951, however, the Army Security Agency (now the NSA) obtained part of a Soviet World War II code book, and found that the Soviets, apparently having run short of code books, had re-used it. This find allowed US code-breakers to decipher sporadic Soviet messages sent from Moscow to its embassy in Washington. They revealed that secret data that the CIA had given to the British had been passed on to Soviet intelligence. The leak had continued into the post-war years. In a series of tense meetings in the Shoreham Hotel, attended by representatives of the FBI, CIA, Army Security Agency, and the British security service, MI-5, British officials admitted that a British diplomat who had served in Washington in 1945 was suspected of being a Soviet agent. His name was Donald Maclean, and he was scheduled to be interrogated.

Three weeks later, on May 25, 1951, Maclean disappeared from London. He turned up in Moscow with another former British intelligence officer, Guy Burgess. Both Burgess and Maclean were Soviet spies. Further, Burgess had been living in Philby's house in Washington and Philby had been told of the investigation. After re-analyzing the Soviet messages, both the CIA and FBI concluded that Maclean and Burgess had had help from a third spy getting information directly from the CIA, and that was probably Philby, and Philby had tipped off Burgess.

British intelligence gradually came to the same conclusion. The problem for British intelligence was that the clues came from secret cryptographic interceptions, and the government held that this evidence could not be revealed. In August 1951, Philby was recalled to London, and after an inconclusive interrogation, was secretly cashiered from MI-6.

Angleton realized that Philby, and the Russians running him as an agent, had used him as an unwitting source for 18 months. A great deal of information had been compromised. At the very minimum, the KGB had been given the CIA's order of battle, and it now knew who was who in American intelligence. He could also assume Philby had provided keen assessments of the strengths and vulnerabilities of many of the CIA's major players, including himself. And Philby had learned much about the CIA's methods, including the ones used to verify the loyalty of its secret sources...

Angleton was therefore not surprised when WIN and the entire "Polish Home Army" turned out to be an intelligence hoax. Had it been a real underground, Philby would have betrayed every element of it to his Soviet controllers. The Soviets would then replace the real agents with fake ones, and use them to channel disinformation to the CIA. When the CIA began checking on WIN through aerial reconnaissance, communication intercepts, and other sources to which Philby was not privy, it found all claims of military victories did not stand up. Moreover, all of the émigré agents put in contact with WIN had disappeared. Since Philby had vetted the files of these agents, it had to be assumed that the identity of these agents was also known to the Soviets. So whatever remained of WIN was under Soviet control. Yet WIN was now requesting that the CIA parachute an American general into Poland to lead the uprising.

Angleton realized it was a trap. He went directly to General Walter Bedell Smith, who was then Director of Central Intelligence (and his trout fishing partner.) He told him WIN was a deception, and that, under no circumstances, should American officers be air dropped into Poland.

Many in the CIA, including Frank Wisner, maintained that WIN was real, in December 1951, despite Philby's betrayal. Then Soviet intelligence decided to itself reveal the operation to embarrass America. The Polish Government broadcast a two hour long radio program on how WIN was a ruse. It explained that the real Polish Home Army had been eliminated by security forces in 1947. In its place had been substituted the fictitious WIN, staffed by Communist officers. It described how Polish security forces had staged mock battles, leaving burnt out tank hulls to be photographed to give WIN credibility, and had used the clandestine radios that the CIA had supplied to supply disinformation. So that there could be no doubt that WIN had been a deception from the outset, the broadcast gave a full accounting of all the money and weapons that had been sent to WIN by the CIA. It said that WIN had used the CIA's gold coins to finance the deception.

By early 1953, the CIA determined that not only was WIN a fraud but so were a half-dozen other supposedly anti-Soviet undergrounds, such as the guerrilla army in the Carpathian Mountains in the Ukraine. Even if they began as real resistance groups, they had been taken over by Soviet intelligence.

The "intelligence" that WIN and other such groups fed the CIA was disinformation. The purpose of the disinformation, as the CIA now read it, was to distract the United States from the real weaknesses in the Soviet system in Eastern Europe, and to focus its attention on fake weaknesses.

Since Wisner and his Office of Policy Coordination had been led disastrously astray by Soviet deception planners, Bedell Smith and his deputy Allen Welsh Dulles decided they needed a new approach to deception. Angleton was assigned the job of analyzing how Soviet intelligence succeeded in falsifying a reality so completely that it sustained the illusion over nearly four years. When Dulles became CIA Director in 1953, he asked Angleton to create a new unit, called the counterintelligence staff that would work directly for the Director. Angleton became its first chief. His mandate was to guard against strategic deceptions. To Angleton this mandate required more than merely uncovering spies and disinformation, it required what he called mirror-thinking, or entering the mind of the adversary intelligence service.

8. Theory of Perfect Deception

Angleton spent the better part of the next decade attempting to unravel the design of his arch rival, the KGB. He re-examined the elements not only that made the WIN deception work in Poland, but which allowed it to go undiscovered. The question he had to answer was how both the CIA and MI6 could have been duped for so long by the Russians. When he interviewed the CIA executives involved, he concluded that part of the problem was institutional arrogance: a belief they could not be duped. As he formulated the problem to Dulles, the success of a deception over time depended on constant fine tuning to keep it credible. WIN succeeded because its planners had constant feedback from Philby. So when parts of the WIN story did not ring true to the CIA or MI-6, they could be adjusted by supplying another false defector or piece of disinformation. This real-time information from inside the CIA, plus institutional arrogance, was what sustained the deception.

Angleton made it his first order of business to create a central registry of all CIA sources in his counterintelligence unit. His staff would then assign each source a label based on whether or not they could be assessed as bona fide. If they could not meet Angleton's standard, the information they supplied could be viewed as disinformation. While this central registry gave Angleton great power over the Soviet Russia division and other intelligence-gathering fiefdoms, it also created enormous friction between his staff and the case officers who were running the sources whose credibility was now routinely questioned.

His concept that the CIA was vulnerable to penetration by the KGB also annoyed CIA officers who had dedicated much of their lives to serving America. They became increasingly antagonistic to having their loyalty become suspect simply because bits of information, which Angleton called "serials," aligned themselves into a pattern" of deception... Even though it yielded few tangible results, Angleton not only persisted in his quest but became increasingly convinced that the Soviet Union, unable to match the military and economic strength of the West, was committed to using deception to win without fighting...

At the heart of strategic deception are disinformation messages. They are designed to cause the target to incorrectly assess a situation. Disinformation messages need not be false. A single message is rarely sufficient to overcome initial suspicions. Messages usually must be orchestrated, as in the WIN ruse, to gradually make the design seem credible. Their reception by the opposition intelligence service cannot be left to chance. They must be dispatched through a channel that it monitors, such as double-agents, compromised codes, and intercepted telephones calls.

So Angleton's theory came down to two lines of communications that hooked up rival intelligence services. Through one line, the disinformation channel, the perpetrator of the deception fed the other intelligence service messages disguised as intelligence. Through the other line, the feedback line, the mole in the intelligence service receiving these messages reports on how they are being assessed, and answers such questions as: Have the messages reached the right parties? Are they believed? Have they been correctly interpreted? Have they been called into question by any unexpected intelligence resource? What additional messages would make them more credible? Once established, these two lines form a loop that allows a deception to be highly effective.

When Angleton learned that Russian behavioral scientists were studying a similar form of "reflexive control" in which subjects' decisions were shaped by adjusting messages to conform to their expectations, he became even more concerned about a deception loop.

9. Enter Golitsyn

By 1961, Angleton's deception theory, as elegant as it was, was foundering on the hard rock of skepticism at the CIA. In addition, his mole hunt had produced bitter enmity that added to doubts about the project. Despite all the work his staff had put into stringing together "serials" and other intelligence morsels into provocative patterns, it had failed to turn up any evidence of an on-going strategic deception. Nor was Angleton able to articulate any grand design behind KGB operations. Then a ray of light came to him from a curious defector in Finland.

On December 22nd 1961, in the midst of a blinding snow storm, a short stocky man, bundled in a heavy overcoat, arrived at the American Embassy in Helsinki. He identified himself as a consul at the Soviet Embassy and asked to see Frank Friberg. The request, coming from a Soviet stranger, set off alarm bells; Friberg was the CIA station chief.

The procedures for dealing with a potential defector were immediately put into effect. After escorting the Russian visitor to an isolated room, the marine guard alerted the desk officer at the embassy, who relayed the "Mayday" message to the CIA station. Within minutes, Friberg rushed down to meet the Soviet walk-in.

The stranger came right to the point. He identified himself as Anatoli Golitsyn, a major in the KGB. To leave no doubt in the mind of his CIA counterpart, he handed over a sheath of secret documents from the files of the Soviet Embassy in Helsinki. He said he would make further information available about the Soviet espionage apparatus if the CIA would immediately arrange his safe passage to the United States, with his wife and daughter.

It was an extraordinary offer. Friberg asked the Russian if he would consider returning to the Soviet Embassy and acting as an agent in place for the CIA.

Golitsyn was adamant. He said he would not survive if he returned. The KGB had means of identifying CIA agents in place -- and he would disclose them after he was safely in America.

Friberg realized he was suggesting that there was a serious leak in the CIA. Unable to persuade him to work as a mole, he asked how much time he had to organize his defection.

Golitsyn said that he had to be out by Christmas. After that, his wife and daughter would be expected back in Moscow, and Soviet security personnel, who were being rotated over the holiday, would be back on active duty. This gave Friberg forty-eight hours.

In Washington, the frantic search through Angleton's central registry of records produced only a single trace on Golitsyn. Peter Derebian, a KGB officer who had been stationed in Vienna before defecting in 1954, had mentioned him to his CIA debriefers as a KGB officer who might be potentially disloyal to the Soviet Union. Before this lead could be followed up in Vienna, Golitsyn had been recalled to Moscow.

The CIA now had a second chance. The Soviet Russia division authorized his immediate evacuation from Helsinki. No matter what diplomatic complications it would cause, it wanted to get this KGB officer in the palm of its hand, and use him to identify, and possibly approach, other potential defectors among Soviet diplomats.

On Christmas, a US Air Force courier plane landed at Helsinki's snow-covered airport. Servicing military attaches stationed abroad, such flights are routinely exempted from foreign customs and immigration inspection. This was, however, not a routine training mission. While the plane waited on the runway, a car pulled up beside it. Its passengers, who carried no luggage, quickly boarded the plane. Among them were Golitsyn, his wife and daughter. Minutes later, the plane was airborne, en route to West Germany.

The first round of interrogations took place at the US Army defector center outside of Frankfurt. Golitsyn was required to write out by hand his entire career in the KGB from the day he joined in 1948 to the day he defected -- listing all the positions he had held, promotions he had received and KGB officers with whom he had come in contact. Unlike most previous defectors, who were field agents with limited knowledge about the central apparatus of the KGB, Golitsyn claimed to have been assigned to the KGB's headquarters in Moscow and also to its "think tank", the KGB institute, where intelligence operations were related to overall Soviet strategy.

To determine if his story was true, Golitsyn was strapped into a stress-analyzing machine, used by the CIA as a lie detector, and quizzed about details of his story -- a process known in the CIA as "fluttering." After each session, counterintelligence experts compared the information he had provided with what was already known. By the end of the first week, the CIA was fully persuaded that he was a bona fide defector who had indeed held the KGB positions he claimed. Arrangements were made to bring him and with his family to the United States.

In February 1962, in an isolated and heavy-guarded CIA compound overlooking the Choptank River in Talbot County, Maryland, he began an extensive debriefing. To the amazement of his debriefers, he not only revealed knowledge of a wide range of secret NATO documents, but identified them by their code numbers. He explained that for convenience the KGB used the NATO numbering system to request specific documents, which would than arrive from its source in France in 72 hours.

President John F. Kennedy, apprised of the Golitsyn revelations, dispatched a personal courier to Paris, with an "eyes only" letter for President Charles De Gaulle. He warned that the KGB had penetrated French intelligence.

A few weeks later, six French intelligence officers, handpicked by De Gaulle, arrived in Washington. They carried with them specially-devised ciphers that bypassed the normal channels of French intelligence, and kept their very presence in the United States a secret from even their own embassy. Their tape-recorded interrogation of Golitsyn, whom they code-named Martel, took 14 days, and left them in a paralyzing quandary.

The French intelligence secrets Golitsyn had provided came from the highest echelon of the French government. When the list of those having access to them was narrowed down to a handful of suspects, suspicion was focused on both the head of French counterintelligence and De Gaulle's personal intelligence advisor.

Golitsyn then dropped another bombshell. He told of a KGB plan he had helped draft in Moscow to use the French intelligence service to spy on missile sites in the American Midwest. French intelligence officers, accredited in Washington, would be ordered by Paris to use their contacts to gather data for the benefit of Moscow. If this was true, it implied that the KGB could use French intelligence officers to the extent that it could use its officers to spy on the United States.

When Angleton informed Philippe de Vosjoli, the French intelligence liaison in Washington, de Vosjoli replied that such an allegation could not be true. Several months later, however, de Vosjoli received an order from Paris to ferret out secret data about American missile bases. Since he knew that France itself had no need for such information about US bases, he asked his superiors for further clarification. The answer instructed him to implement the plan without further delay or questions.

At this point, de Vosjoli became convinced that Golitsyn had actually seen this plan being prepared in Moscow, as he claimed in his debriefing, and that the KGB had fully penetrated French intelligence. He again attempted to warn De Gaulle. Meanwhile, a top French official, who was identified through Golitsyn's leads as a member of a spy ring, died after falling out a window. De Vosjoli believed he was murdered to protect others in the ring. By November 1963, he learned from a friend that his own life was in jeopardy and, with Angleton's assistance, defected to the United States.

The Soviet Russia division meanwhile found Golitsyn difficult to debrief further. When shown pictures of Soviet diplomats, he grew short-tempered, shouting at one point at Pete Bagley, "What good is knowing all the names in the KGB if you don't understand what they do?"

Bagley then asked Golitsyn if he would be willing to personally contact former KGB acquaintances on behalf of the CIA, which is a standard recruitment technique. Golitsyn refused, saying it was pointless since "the KGB knows all your operations in advance." Adding insult to injury, he cited 3 secret CIA attempts to recruit Soviet diplomats in Switzerland and Austria.

Golitsyn then said that he did not want to reveal any further information until he spoke to President Kennedy himself. When informed by Bagley that such an audience was impossible, he said he wanted to leave America and go to England. The Soviet Russia division, unable to deal with him, sent him to London, where MI-6 continued his debriefing.

Golitsyn's stay in England was unexpectedly brief. During his interrogation about the KGB agents in British intelligence, he alluded to a similar penetration in the CIA's Soviet Russia Division. Arthur Martin, the top interrogator in MI-5, zeroed in on the CIA questioning of him.

Golitsyn told Martin that his interrogators in the Soviet Russia Division persisted in asking the wrong questions. He said he was not surprised by this flawed interrogation because he had learned in Moscow that the KGB had recruited at least one, and possibly more, CIA officers in the Soviet Russia Division as moles.

Such a potent allegation could not be ignored. If there was a penetration in the CIA, it would compromise MI-6, MI-5 and other allied intelligence services. Martin decided to go directly to Angleton.

Angleton agreed with him that Golitsyn's CIA debriefing had been mishandled by the Soviet Russia Division. He went to Richard Helms, and made an unprecedented request. He wanted his counterintelligence staff to take over the Golitsyn case.

Helms not only agreed but gave Angleton authority to use whatever resources he needed. By doing so, he set in motion the longest and most contentious debriefing in the history of the CIA.

In July 1963, through a leak arranged by MI-5, the Daily Telegraph in London revealed that Golitsyn (under the purposely misspelled name "Dolitson") was in England. MI-5 then informed Golitsyn that his security had been compromised and arrangements were being made to send him back to the United States. In August, he met with Angleton who told him there would be no more showing him pictures of Soviet diplomats. Angleton told him he wanted to know about the "logic of Soviet penetration."

Angleton saw it not as a conventional debriefing, but as an "elicitation." They dined and drank together and discussed politics into the early hours of the morning. He even allowed Golitsyn to review copies of his staff's "serials" (though they were scrubbed clean of any names.) To further build confidence, Angleton arranged for Golitsyn to brief Attorney General Robert F. Kennedy on the KGB.

He took him on trips to Europe and Israel to speak to Western intelligence executives. He even discussed with Golitsyn an idea for organizing a new counterintelligence service that would be independent of the CIA.

For his part, Golitsyn furnished Angleton convincing evidence that CIA secrets had been systematically leaked to the KGB. At one point, he recalled in "astonishing detail," according to Angleton, an entire section of the CIA debriefing report on a KGB officer who had defected in 1955. Angleton's staff then traced the handling of the secret report. They found it had been hand-delivered from Vienna to Washington, and its contents had been available only to a handful of CIA officers, including two case officers that handled the defection, their superior at the Vienna CIA station, two officers on the counterintelligence staff who vetted the defector, and two other analysts before the report was "sanitized" for more general distribution. If the KGB had gotten the original version of the debriefing, it must have been from one of these men.

Golitsyn also described an aborted CIA plan to contact a Polish diplomat in Switzerland, alleging that the KGB had been tipped off. Checking the dates and personnel involved, Angleton's staff found that the operation had been planned precisely as Golitsyn had described. How could the KGB have had such good information about an operation not carried out? Angleton concluded that someone involved in the planning of this recruitment was responsible for this leak. This narrowed down the suspects to officers and executives in the Soviet Russia Division.

More specifically, Golitsyn claimed that the KGB had been managing the career of a CIA employee code-named "Sacha." According to Golitsyn, they had "promoted him in the CIA" by providing him with successes. These successes were the names of minor agents in Germany he could "burn" and take credit for exposing. Angleton assembled a task force from his own staff, the FBI, and the Office of Security to pursue this lead and an FBI espionage expert to re-examine the files of CIA officers who had been promoted because of successful cases. "Sacha," however, was never found.

After analyzing Angleton's serials, Golitsyn said that "Sacha" could not account for all the leaks. He argued that the KGB had to have more than a single mole, using the analogy of a growing "cancer" that a patient refused to cut out.

Intensifying the mole hunt, Angleton planted a series of "marked cards" in the Soviet Russia Division. One of these "marked cards" concerned an operation by the Royal Mounted Police in Ottawa to recruit a Soviet diplomat accredited to Canada. If there was a leak, Angleton expected that the KGB would put the diplomat under surveillance, which would in turn by seen by Canadian counterintelligence. When Angleton then learned that the marked card had indeed reached the KGB, and the diplomat was being tailed, it further convinced him that, as Golitsyn had insisted, there was a mole in the Soviet Russia division.

When Angleton reported the playing out of the marked cards to Helms, who had become Director of Central Intelligence in 1966, Helms told that this was a no-win "nightmare scenario." After Philby's flight to Moscow in January 1963, there was no longer any doubt about the KGB's capabilities, but he had hoped that the damage could be contained. Angleton convinced him that the KGB had learned some CIA secrets. The issue was how. Some of it could have come from intercepted communications, surveillance of CIA agents, leaks garnered from the public domain, or even shrewd guesses, but the fact that the KGB had learned the names, dates, and details of secret operations that had not been carried out had to be decisively dealt with.

Helms authorized the Office of Security to distribute different marked cards to six separate compartments in the Soviet Russia Division. When the Office of Security reported back that the marked cards that turned up in Soviet hands came from more than one compartment, he accepted Angleton's view that there was a penetration.

His next step was randomly transferring some of the personnel out of the compartments that had leaked, which meant the careers of possibly innocent officers were ruined. Angleton then arranged new rounds of marked cards to test those who remained. This turned out to be far more time-consuming than had been anticipated. Evaluating the results of each marked card experiment took months of counterintelligence work. So the mole hunt dragged on for seven years. In the course of it, no fewer than five top CIA officers in the Soviet Russia Division became suspect and were re-assigned to less sensitive positions in other divisions, moves that led to confusion, demoralization, and, by the late 1960s, near paralysis of intelligence gathering.

In 1968, Helms called in Angleton. He told him that he had given him all the resources he had requested to develop the Golitsyn story, and he expected "an elephant." He asked him point-blank: Had Golitsyn come up with the KGB's deception plans?

Angleton replied that Golitsyn had been one of a small of young analysts in a KGB "think tank" who prepared the plans for the massive reorganization of Soviet intelligence that took place in 1959. Aleksandr Shelepin, who then became Chairman of the KGB, said that the KGB would focus on manipulating the actions of the United States.

"That was a decade ago," Helms shot back. "We need a briefing on what specifics he has to offer."

Angleton had Golitsyn meet with a group of experts that Helms had assembled. Golitsyn began by saying that he had not, or ever claimed to, participate, in the Kremlin's high-level deception planning. But he had attended lectures on it and drawn together various pieces of the mosaic from sources inside the KGB. But when pressed by the experts about his theories, he shouted back demanding to know what evidence they had for disputing his theories. The meeting ended acrimoniously because he became "overly defensive," according to Angleton. The next day, Helms told Angleton his experts were unimpressed. He ordered him to put Golitsyn "on ice" and allow the CIA's Soviet Russia Division "do its job."

Golitsyn retired to Florida, where over the next decade he wrote a 1200 page manuscript based on material he had assembled for the Helms briefing. When Angleton made it available for me to read years later, I could not follow all the convoluted twists in the labyrinth that he claimed was the Soviet intelligence apparatus.

Golitsyn's thesis is that in 1959 the KGB had been reorganized into two parts: an inner and an outer KGB. The inner unit did the strategic deception planning but none of its officers were allowed to have contact with Western intelligence. The outer unit, which was in constant contact with the West through dangles, double agent games and recruitment attempts, carried out the operations but it had no knowledge of its strategic design and no contact with the inner circle. In that way, if anyone in the outer unit defected or was recruited by the West, he could reveal tactical but not strategic secrets. Golitsyn traced out, in excruciating detail, the multitudinous preparations that had to be made in the Soviet Government, the Communist Party, the KGB, and foreign liaison services to facilitate the 1959 reorganization. He described, layer by layer, its different parts, personnel transferred to it, and the cover stories that were used as a smokescreen. What was missing was any specific KGB deception plan.

10. The Cuban Warning

The success of case officers in the CIA depends heavily on the sources and other assets they recruit. If they turn out to be reliable, the CIA officers are heroes and rise within the organization. But if they are discredited, or prove to be double-agents, it may undermine their career. This put Angleton in a precarious position within the bureaucracy since after the Philby debacle, it was his job to test the bona fides of the assets on whom case officers in other division often had staked their careers. In the early 1960s, Angleton, aside from nearly paralyzing the operations of the Soviet Russia division, had turned his scrutiny on the Western Hemisphere division, and Desmond FitzGerald, the CIA executive in charge of the agency's covert war on Castro's Cuba. FitzGerald was also a man with such good social connections to the family of President John FitzGerald Kennedy that many at the CIA mistakenly believed he was a distant relative. What brought Angleton in direct conflict with him was a Cuban named Roland Cubela (code-named AMLASH) that FitzGerald's division had recruited to assassinate Castro.

In 1963, after a CIA-sponsored coup d'état against Castro had failed to materialize, FitzGerald came under increasing pressure from President Kennedy and Attorney General Kennedy to get rid of Castro. The opportunity came in early September in Port Alegre, Brazil where Cubela had been sent to represent Castro at the Pan American Games. Cubela had offered to assassinate a Cuban official for the CIA a year earlier, but when he refused to take a lie detector test the CIA had severed contact with him.

Now FitzGerald received permission to re-activate him since he had access to Castro. On September 7th, FitzGerald dispatched Nestor Sanchez to Brazil to ask Cubela if he was willing to carry out an elimination mission aimed at Castro. Cubela agreed on one condition: he wanted a personal meeting with either Attorney General Robert F. Kennedy or a high-ranking official of the Kennedy Administration. He said this meeting was necessary because he wanted to make certain that President Kennedy had authorized this move against Castro.

As extraordinary as this request was, FitzGerald, decided that as a friend of the Attorney General, he would go to meet the assassin. The contact plan for the meeting noted: "FitzGerald will represent himself as a personal representative of Robert F. Kennedy who traveled to [Paris] for specific purpose of meeting AMLASH and giving him assurances of full support with the change of the present government." FitzGerald used the alias "James Clark," but he was physically recognizable from press photographs as a social friend in the Kennedy circle.

The meeting took place in a hotel room in Paris on October 29, 1963. FitzGerald was accompanied by Nestor Sanchez, who wrote in his report, "FitzGerald informed Cubela that the United States is prepared to render all necessary assistance to any anti-communist Cuban group which succeeds in neutralizing the present Cuban leadership." They discussed, in this regard, eliminating Castro. Cubela asked for a high-powered rifle with a telescopic sight -- the same type of weapon Oswald would use 23 days later in Dallas.

After that meeting, Fitzgerald authorized Sanchez to supply Cubela with a weapon that would provide better cover. It was a Papermate ballpoint pen with one hidden enhancement: a tiny needle that released a lethal toxin. The poison, Blackleaf 40, could be either injected into a beverage Castro might drink or, as it was transdermal, put on an object Castro might touch. Cubela, after surreptitiously administering the poison, could then discard the innocent-looking pen.

Meanwhile, Angleton's counterintelligence staff developed serious concerns about Cabala's provenance. Ray Rocca, who obsessively researched anomalies for Angleton, came upon an intriguing coincidence: Cubela had been recruited for the mission in Brazil to assassinate Castro on September 7, and a day later, Castro had gone to Brazilian embassy in Havana, to tell an American AP reporter that he knew the American government was behind plots to kill him. Rocca pointed out that there was no record of Castro ever before giving an interview in the Brazilian embassy. Angleton, as he later told me, did not believe in such coincidences: he reckoned Castro knew about the meeting in Brazil, and was sending a message that he knew about the CIA's plot. In Angleton's scenario, it was a distinct possibility that Cubela was an agent provocateur, whom Castro dangled to the CIA to ascertain if President Kennedy had authorized his assassination. The danger was clear to Angleton: By working with Cubela, FitzGerald could give Castro evidence of the involvement of the highest echelon of American government in the assassination plot. He warned Fitzgerald that he considered the operation "insecure," and suggested it be terminated.

But FitzGerald had gone further than Angleton knew. To further convince Cubela that the President had authorized the elimination of Castro, FitzGerald wrote a "signal" into a Presidential speech, a phrase that described the Castro regime as a "small band of conspirators" that needed to be "removed." When President Kennedy delivered those very words in a speech in Miami on November 18th, if Cubela was a double agent, as Angleton suspected, Castro would have his proof.

The next meeting with Cubela took place in Paris on November 22nd 1963. Cubela was given the assassination pen, but the news President Kennedy had been assassinated ended the meeting -- and the plot. On June 23rd 1965, as further evidence developed that Cubela had been compromised, Helms ordered all contact with him ended. For Angleton, this was confirmation that Cubela's role in the plot to assassinate Castro had been monitored, if not orchestrated by Castro's intelligence service. But being right about Fitzgerald's bad judgment did not make Angleton popular within the CIA the implication was that a misguided CIA assassination attempt may have set in motion the events in Dallas.

Part Three

THE FALL OF ANGLETON

11. The White Feathers

In January 1973, Richard Helms, who had been Angleton's greatest supporter, was fired by Nixon in the midst of the Watergate crises, and sent to Iran as US Ambassador. Angleton now knew his own days were numbered. Colby, the new executive director, made no secret of his animosity towards Angleton. He went to the new Director, James Schlesinger, who had been Nixon's budget director, and told him that it was imperative that Angleton be fired.

Schlesinger called Angleton into his office. He went through Colby's case against him point by point. He told him that Colby's view was that Angleton's conspiratorial approach had confused and weakened the CIA. Despite his past service, he was now "more of a liability than an asset."

Angleton made no effort to rebut this attack. He recognized that he had paralyzed part of the CIA, and, assuming he had been fired, stood up and prepared to leave the room, Schlesinger then asked him, almost as a courtesy, what he himself viewed as the difficulty at the CIA.

Angleton said deferentially that he doubted that the Director had the time to have him lay out these issues. But Schlesinger told him he had all afternoon, and beckoned him to sit down. Angleton then told him that "an intelligence service is most vulnerable to deception when it considers itself invulnerable to deception." He proceeded to lay out what he called the "nightmare scenario" in which, because of the CIA's propensity towards denying it was vulnerable, the KGB could penetrate both the FBI and CIA. That would allow it to mount successful deceptions that could influence the way the President acted.

When Angleton emerged from the Director's office 3 hours later, not only he had not been fired but he was now his confidant.

Angleton's reprieve was short lived. Schlesinger served only four months in the CIA. His replacement was William Colby. Colby made no secret of his antipathy towards Angleton (who had once investigated Colby's contact in Saigon with a suspected Russian agent). But aside from his personal animosity towards him, he believed Angleton's thinking was dead wrong. He described his mole hunt as based on paranoia. As far as he was concerned, "the function of the CIA was to penetrate the Kremlin not protect itself against the KGB." Angleton's mole hunt was interfering with this offensive function. He was willing to rely for defense against KGB infiltration on the agency's tried and tested security procedures, such as periodic polygraph examinations. He was convinced, he told me, that Angleton's methods were "counterproductive."

Colby moved quickly to end Angleton's power. He began by drastically reducing his counterintelligence staff of 180 officers. He ended its job of determining the bona fides of sources, which also ended its leverage over the Soviet Russia Division. He also eliminated its liaison duty with Israel's Mossad and other long term foreign allies of Angleton. This reorganization made the counterintelligence staff largely superfluous to the work of the CIA.

Colby then found a way to neatly dispose of Angleton himself. He called investigative reporter Seymour Hersh into his office in late December 1974, and told him that before he became its Director, the CIA had been involved in an illicit mail opening program that intercepted letters mailed from the Soviet Union to American citizens. He further told Hersh that Angleton had been responsible for it. In fact, Angleton had been only nominally responsible for the program. Now Hersh had his story and culprit.

Finally, on December 20, 1974, Colby completed the coup by summoning Angleton to his office and informing him that Hersh was about to break a story in the New York Times that would expose the mail opening program and name him. The ensuing scandal would end Angleton's usefulness at the CIA so Colby asked for and received Angleton's immediate resignation. Angleton left the CIA on Christmas Eve, never to return,

The purge had other casualties, including his long time associates Rocca and Miler, and many other people who had worked with Angleton for decades. Within days, the "serials" that the counter-intelligence staff had amassed over 20 years were systematically shredded. With Angleton gone, the CIA's Soviet Russia Division re-opened the recruitment floodgates. It was back in the espionage business.

After his departure, Angleton fashioned three white feathers, as symbols of cowardice. He planned to give to them to the three top CIA executives under Colby, who had actually authorized the mail opening program. They had allowed Angleton to take the blame. But he never sent them. Instead, he used them as fishing lures when he went on a long solitary salmon fishing expedition on the Matapedia River in New Brunswick, Canada.

12. The Fisherman

Angleton spent most of 1975 in Tucson and in the Arizona desert. He took with him his collection of over two hundred fishing lures, some of them given to him by Bedell Smith in the early days of the CIA, but most of them painstakingly designed by him. Like all lures, they were meant to misrepresent reality in a way that would trigger a response in the target, making him a formidable fly fisherman. He missed his prize winning orchids in Washington and the Virginia greenhouse he had designed. So he returned to Washington. He also needed to testify before Congressional sub-committees investigating the CIA.

On November 9, 1979, the US embassy in Tehran was seized by Iranian students. A large trove of partially-shredded CIA documents were captured, and published in 60 volumes by the Iranian government. Among them were a set of top secret directives sent to the CIA station in Tehran (as well as other CIA operation centers) that appeared to bear directly on the Angleton affair.

Up until 1973, these directives warned CIA field officers against Soviet provocations in which the KGB sent Russian diplomats, codenamed by the CIA "redtops," to offer their services to the CIA. The purpose of such "dangles" was to lead the CIA on a wild goose chase. For example, "Director of Central Intelligence Directive 4/2," states: "The establishment of bona fides of disaffected persons will be given particular attention because of the demonstrated use of defector channels by hostile services to penetrate or convey false or deceptive information to U.S. Intelligence services." Other directives cited findings that "REDTOP services have been using sophisticated and serious walk-ins as a provocation technique." These warnings reflected Angleton's view that the KGB orchestrated deceptions to throw the CIA off balance.

But after Helms turned temporary control over to Colby in January 1973, a new directive ordered a different approach. "We have concluded that we do ourselves a disservice if we shy away from promising cases because of fear of provocation." it asserted. "We are confident that we are capable of determining whether or not a producing agent is supplying bona fide information."

This directive effectively freed CIA field officers to recruit REDTOPs before the counterintelligence staffed determined their bona fides. It assumed that the value of a "producing agent" could be established from the information he furnished without an investigation of his bona fides. These new directives expressed confidence that the CIA could use these REDTOP volunteers as "resident agents" in Moscow and advised all stations: "We have the capability to mount and support such operations over an indefinite period, and we currently are able to exfiltrate agents, in most cases with their families, from the REDTOP countries when it is time for them to leave." Clearly, the CIA now believed it could deal with the KGB, even in Moscow, even with untested recruits. But what had led the CIA to have this new confidence?

To find out, I arranged to meet Angleton at the Army Navy Club in Washington in 1984. He chose the venue because he took pride in the fact that he had held the rank of Major in the Army, which qualified him for membership. After a leisurely lunch, I showed him the relevant passages in these CIA directives, which he said he was "all too familiar with." He said that "clearly the CIA had changed its appreciation of the KGB."

"Had there been a coup d'état at the CIA?" I asked.

"It was more a coup de grâce," he replied.

He explained that in fields of scientific investigation, such as biology, the investigator can safely assume that what he sees through a microscope has not been put there for his benefit, but in the field of secret intelligence, an investigator cannot make that assumption. Spies, unlike microbes, do attempt to dupe outsiders. Yet the new policy, as reflected in these directives, was based on the idea that the deception problem could be solved by the data itself. If it dove-tailed with other information, and was useful, it could be deemed to be "productive intelligence."

Angleton said Colby strongly believed that the CIA had the technological ability to weed out disinformation with its satellites, computers, and polygraphs. "I disagreed with him, but I lost the battle."

Three years later, Angleton lost another battle. He died of lung cancer.

Part Four

WAS ANGLETON RIGHT?

13. The Mole Question

In the bitter debate in American intelligence, no one seriously doubted that the KGB had made major efforts to recruit moles in Western intelligence services. How could they not have? The KGB had penetrated MI5 and MI6 in England with spies such as Burgess, Maclean, and Philby, as well as services in West Germany, France, Italy, Canada, and other NATO allies. It had also recruited spies in the US military, such as Lieutenant Colonel William Henry Whalen, while he served as the intelligence advisor to the Army Chief of Staff, and the National Security Agency, such as Bernon Mitchell, William Martin, Ronald Pelton, Jack E. Dunlap, and Robert Lipka, all of whom comprised secrets ciphers. But, as of Angleton's firing in 1975, US counterintelligence was unable to discover a single case of the KGB recruiting a CIA officer as a mole. (One CIA clerk, William Kampiles, tossed CIA documents over the wall of the Soviet Embassy in Athens, but he had not been recruited by the KGB, and turned himself in to US authorities.) Of course, what is successfully hidden is, by definition, not found. So either the KGB had the means to keep their moles invisible from the CIA, or, as Colby had contended, there was no penetration of the CIA. The new CIA pointed to the latter alternative as proof that Angleton had become unhinged from reality, and that became the conventional wisdom, at least up until 1994.

On February 24, 1994 Aldrich Ames was arrested by the FBI on the charge of spying for the Soviet Union and Russia while he was employed by the CIA. He pleaded guilty and was sentenced to life imprisonment. Ames admitted to having worked for the KGB for 10 years. During part of his employment as a KGB mole, he had been the head of the CIA's Soviet Russia Division's counterintelligence unit. From this vantage point, Ames could feed back to the KGB the CIA's evaluation of the information it was receiving from Russian "dangles" and dispatched agents as well as that from actual spies. The KGB thus had the feedback loop that Angleton had described. The fact that Ames passed his polygraph exams for a decade undercut the idea that these machines were proof against deception. That Ames had managed to rise to be head of the CIA's Soviet counterintelligence unit despite his reportedly lackluster performance and, at the same time, avoid all the CIA's security defenses, showed that the KGB had the ability to manage his career within the CIA. This feat raised the issue of whether the KGB had other resources in the CIA. (The FBI subsequently discovered another CIA officer, Harold Nicholson, was a mole for the Soviet intelligence service, but he only began his work after Ames was captured.)

Angleton was also right when he warned CIA Director Schlesinger about the vulnerability of the FBI to KGB penetration, a warning that infuriated FBI Director J. Edgar Hoover. The proof came in February 2001. Robert Hanssen, a high-level FBI officer, was arrested for selling American intelligence secrets to Russia. He admitted that he had been working as a KGB mole for over two decades. On 6 July 2001, he pleaded guilty to thirteen counts of espionage, and he was sentenced, like Ames, to life imprisonment. During much of his 22 year career as a KGB mole, he had worked in counterintelligence where he had a responsibility for monitoring KGB operations. Since the FBI has the responsibility for investigating all KGB recruitments in the United States, even if they occur in the CIA, NSA, or military, he could monitor all of America's efforts to counter KGB espionage, and keep the KGB abreast of this investigation. He also had access to the FBI computer system. Each investigation widened his access. For example, when the CIA was investigating the leaks that eventually led to Ames, the FBI, and Hanssen, had a "need to know" about all the secret operations that had been compromised by that leak. The feedback he was able to provide to the KGB enabled the KGB not only to eliminate the real sources the CIA was getting information from in Russia, but also to substitute for them disinformation agents. And then through Ames (and possibly other moles in the CIA), it could determine if the disinformation worked, and, if it didn't, modify it. The double long-term penetration in the FBI and CIA confirmed Angleton's nightmare of a sustainable deception loop.

These two mole cases demonstrated that the KGB clearly had

the ability to recruit, career-manage, service, coordinate, protect, and utilize the intelligence product of moles in both the CIA and FBI for a long period of time. It was the conceit that the CIA and FBI were invulnerable to penetration, not the suspicion that the KGB could penetrate these agencies that turned out to be out of touch with reality.

14. The Deception Question

Even Angleton's harshest critics at the CIA, such as William Colby, recognized that the KGB planted misleading clues in intelligence channels. But they believed, as Colby wrote in directives, that the CIA was able to weed out such tactical disinformation by considering it in the context of intelligence gathered by satellites, communications intercepts, and other sources. This view held that while it might be possible to temporarily confuse CIA field officers, disinformation would never be passed up the chain to the White House. Angleton's view that it could be used to manipulate a President was peremptorily dismissed. Colby termed it "sick think."

In 1995, however, the CIA Inspector General found that in the 1980s and early 1990s the KGB had dispatched at least half-dozen double agents who provided disinformation cooked up in Moscow to their CIA case officers. It further discovered that this concoction of bogus and factually true information had routinely been passed between 1986 and 1994 to three Presidents -- President Ronald Reagan, President George H.W. Bush and President Bill Clinton. The disinformation, according to the Inspector General, became part of one of the CIA's most highly classified products, with each report signed personally by the CIA director, provided with a distinctive blue stripe to signify their importance, and sent directly to the President, Secretary of Defense and Secretary of State. When the CIA Inspector General retrospectively traced out the path of this disinformation in the blue border reports, he found that the "senior CIA officers responsible for these reports had known that some of their sources were controlled by Russian intelligence." These CIA officials apparently continued to forward the Russian disinformation to the White House because it would be too embarrassing for them to admit that they had been so badly deceived.

Whatever their motive, the CIA officers who had been gulled by the KGB found a common interest with the KGB in not revealing on-going deception. The CIA Director John Deutch, who had received these blue border reports when he was deputy director of the Department of Defense, told Congress that the CIA's failure to disclose that the intelligence was from KGB-controlled agents was "an inexcusable lapse in elementary intelligence practice."

So Angleton proved to be right about the KGB's capabilities to penetrate, deceive, and use the CIA to deceive its own government.

15. R.I.P

By the time Angleton died, in 1987, the term Angletonian had become an adjective used to describe something conspiratorial, overly paranoid, or bizarre. Even though every Director of Central Intelligence from Allan Dulles to James Schlesinger kept Angleton as their key advisor on counterintelligence, his critics ridiculed his idea that KGB moles could infiltrate the FBI and CIA. In the media, the notion of moles was treated as evidence of his paranoia. Simply put, in 1987, Angleton's thesis that the KGB could use the CIA to deceive Presidents was viewed by almost every commentator on the subject as an excursion into paranoia.

In Russia, however a handful of people in the KGB and Kremlin had a very different appreciation of the situation. They knew in 1987, as the FBI would only learn many years later, that the CIA had been successfully penetrated. The KGB had advanced its mole Aldrich Ames to a key position in the heart of its counterintelligence. They also knew that the FBI, America's anti-espionage service, had also been doubly penetrated. The KGB had two moles, Earl Edwin Pitts and Robert Hanssen, with access to the FBI's computer files. They also knew that these moles were reporting back to Moscow the thinking of American counterintelligence. So the KGB had installed the feedback part of the deception loop. They also knew that the KGB had no fewer than six disinformation agents. From their feedback, they knew that the CIA and FBI had accepted them as reliable sources. These agents formed the disinformation part of the loop. They also knew that their Moscow-prepared disinformation was moving from the CIA case officers, to the Reports section. And that it was included in the reports signed by the National Intelligence Officer for Soviet Russia and Director of Central Intelligence William Casey (and then William Webster) for the eyes of President Ronald Reagan, Secretary of State George Shultz, and Secretary of Defense Caspar Weinberger.

After the Cold War ended, the CIA learned more about this vulnerability. In 2004, KGB Col. Victor Cherkashin, spoke at a dinner in his honor at the Spy Museum in Washington about how the KGB duped the CIA. He recounted to former US intelligence officers how he helped run two KGB moles -- one well-placed in the CIA's Soviet Russia Division, the other in the FBI -- when he was deputy KGB chief at the Soviet Embassy in Washington in the 1980s. They were of course Aldrich Ames and Robert Hanssen. He explained how this helped facilitate the KGB's disinformation operations to further delude the CIA even after leaks were detected by the CIA. Of course, by this time, the CIA Inspector General had already found out about the KGB's success in deception. Cherkashin could gloat in 2004 over the KGB's prior successes because the CIA leadership had not seen that Angleton had been right.

***

Appendix

THE WILDERNESS OF MIRRORS

I. The Cold War Moles

In July 1977, President Jimmy Carter's secret Special Coordinating Committee, the White House unit that oversees the clandestine activities of the CIA, received a piece of dismaying news: A Central Intelligence Agency spy in the Kremlin, "Trianon," had been apprehended by the K.G.B., the Soviet intelligence service. In 1978, the Soviet press reported that this American spy had been tried for treason and sentenced to death.

"Trianon" was the code name for Anatoly N. Filatov, a 37-year-old aide in the Soviet Foreign Ministry. The CIA had caught him in a sex trap in Algiers in 1976, when he was attached to the Soviet Embassy in Algeria. After being confronted with compromising photographs, Filatov was persuaded or blackmailed, as he is reported to have claimed at his trial, to work as a spy for the CIA when he was reassigned to the Foreign Ministry in Moscow. He was supplied with all the necessary paraphernalia for espionage: a miniature camera for photographing secret documents, a "burst" transmitter signaling his contact in the American Embassy in Moscow, and a "dead drop" on a Moscow bridge, where he could inconspicuously leave his microfilm for American intelligence agents to pick up.

How he was so quickly caught by the K.G.B. has been a mystery of immense concern to US intelligence. Was he detected through routine Soviet surveillance? Was he exposed by an accidental leak from American intelligence? Or was he betrayed by a mole planted inside American intelligence?

In response to a request from Senator Daniel Patrick Moynihan, Democrat of New York, and Senator Malcolm Wallop, Republican of Wyoming, the Senate Select Committee on Intelligence conducted an investigation into the circumstances that led to Filatov's exposure, which itself opened up a Pandora's Box of secrets about the spy war.

When the Senate Select Committee on Intelligence was briefed on the Filatov case shortly after his arrest in 1977, according to one staff member of the committee, it found that the case had thrown the American intelligence community into confusion. Consternation arose because Filatov was apparently the only United States agent in a position of access to secrets in the Soviet Union - he was, in the language of the intelligence world, a "mole." Moreover, incredible as it may seem, he may have been the only mole that the CIA had established inside the Kremlin in more than a decade. According to one high Government official, who was familiar with the major CIA operations between 1969 and 1977, the CIA failed to establish a single productive mole in the Soviet Union between the arrest of Col. Oleg Penkovsky in Moscow in 1962 and the recruitment of Filatov in 1976. This intelligence gap was also cited by former CIA executives and a staff member of the Senate Select Committee on Intelligence.

The only exceptions mentioned by these sources were two Soviet Unite Nations diplomats - codenamed "Top Hat" and "Fedora," recruited by the FBI in New York and a Soviet diplomat codenamed "Igor," recruited by the CIA in Washington, during the 1960s. In all three cases, however, CIA counterintelligence assessed that they were double agent working for the K.G.B., and, in any case, all three returned to Moscow and cut off their contacts to the CIA.

The primary task of any clandestine intelligence service, whether the CIA or the K.G.B., is to establish moles within the enemy's inner sanctum that are in a position to warn changes in its plans and intentions. "No intelligence can function unless it has secret sources," Richard Helms, a former Director of Central Intelligence, pointed out to me.

There are, be sure, other profitable ways of gathering intelligence, such as overhead surveillance of a potential enemy's activities, tapping into its underwater cables by submarines and the interception of communications by powerful antennae. Such reconnaissance requires highly sophisticated equipment, such as spy planes, satellites, underwater robots and computers, but it does not require the operation of clandestine service. And, even in the age of satellites and electronic wizardry, clandestine services are deemed necessary to report on the strategic thinking of an adversary and other clues that cannot be intercepted by remote platform. The clandestine service specializes in the spotting, compromising, recruiting and handling of moles on a regular basis. This is called Human intelligence, or in CIA-talk, HUMINT.

While public debate over the CIA, fueled by Presidential inquiries and Congressional investigations, has narrowly focused on the charge that the agency has abused its power by spying on domestic groups outside its legal purview, the secret concern in intelligence circles, which has not surfaced in any of the many public hearings, is that the CIA is not spying effectively on its principal adversary: the Soviet bloc. As William Harris, a counterintelligence expert from the RAND Corporation put the question: "Why has the CIA repeatedly failed to penetrate the Soviet system by recruiting agents?"

Within the CIA itself, this question has been the center of a bitter and destructive debate that has persisted unresolved for some 20 years. On one side of the issue, it is argued that the K.G.B. has successfully established its own moles with the CIA and other US intelligence services, and that these moles report to Moscow the secret plans and sources of the CIA, thereby making it impossible for the CIA to recruit, or keep secret its own moles.

Tennent Bagley, who was the deputy chief of the CIA's Soviet Bloc Division in the mid-1960's and was responsible for countering the activities of Soviet intelligence, explained to me that "it takes a mole to catch a mole." According to his view, the two most successful moles that the CIA ever recruited, Col. Peter Popov (1953-58) and Colonel Penkovsky (1961-62), were both caught by Soviet intelligence because they had been betrayed by a K.G.B. mole, or moles, working in American intelligence. Bagley claimed, moreover, to have seen during his tenure in the CIA direct evidence of a mole "feeding back," as he put it, operational plans of the CIA to the K.G.B. "In one case, Soviet intelligence clearly knew about an elaborate CIA plan to recruit a Soviet-bloc diplomat in Switzerland," he pointed out. He knew of no productive mole that the CIA had recruited in the Soviet Union since the capture of Penkovsky in 1962. (Bagley retired from the CIA in 1972.) He accounted for this failure in blunt terms: "It is impossible for the CIA to maintain any secret sources if it is penetrated."

This argument was carried much farther by James Jesus Angleton, who served as the CIA's counterintelligence chief until 1975. Angleton, theorizing on the basis of information supplied by Soviet defectors, believed that he had pinpointed the K.G.B. "Penetrations," as he called them, in the Soviet Bloc Division Of the CIA In 1963, he began purging or transferring four possible suspects. When these "administrative measures," as he called them, did not result in ferreting out the mole or plugging the apparent leak, Angleton took more drastic action. In 1960s, he explained to me, he completely "cut off" the entire Soviet Bloc Division from information about highly sensitive cases. This step led to the near paralysis of the Soviet Bloc Division, which was then responsible for all CIA intelligence activities in the Soviet Union and Eastern Europe.

On the other side of the debate, a large number of CIA officers, such as William Colby, who became Director of Central Intelligence in 1973, who believed that the mole issue was divisive, demoralizing and ultimately a dangerous distraction. They argued that Popov, Penkovsky and other CIA moles were caught by the K.G.B. either through routine surveillance procedures or because of a blunder or mishap in American intelligence - and not through any information supplied by a mole. These intelligence officers viewed the deductive search for moles as "sick think," as Jack Maury, a former head of the CIA's Soviet Bloc Division, described it to me. Indeed, William Colby blamed the failure of the CIA to recruit agents in the Soviet Union on the mistaken fear that there was a mole in the CIA who would quickly betray them. When he became Director, he fired Angleton and transferred other counterintelligence officers who had worked under him. He also did away with the tight compartmentalization' of information that Angleton had insist Colby explains in his autobiography that he took these actions because he believed that Angleton's "ultra conspiratorial turn of mind had, at least in recent years, become more of a liability than an asset to the agency."

The dismissal of Angleton did not end the debate. When the K.G.B. uncovered Filatov, the CIA again had to come to grips with the possibility that Soviet intelligence had a source in the agency. Even though CIA officials told the Senate Select Committee on Intelligence that Filatov's detection had come about because of an inadvertent statement to the press by one of national security adviser Zbigniew Brzezinski's deputies on the National Security Council, a number of counterintelligence officers believed that Filatov had been betrayed by a mole in the CIA.

In fact, the CIA had cogent evidence in its files testifying in no uncertain terms to the capacity of Soviet intelligence to recruit and sustain moles in highly sensitive positions in American and other Western intelligence services. In the early 1960's, the CIA uncovered, through the services of its own anonymous spy, a well organized complex of Soviet moles that included not only American but also French, German, Israeli, British, Swedish and NATO officers.

Most of these agents, according to their public admissions, were induced to work for the K.G.B. by financial rewards or sexual blackmail rather than an ideological sympathy with Communism. Some were enlisted under "false flag" arrangements in which, for example, former Nazis were recruited by a K.G.B. front that Pretended to be a secret Nazi conspiracy. They all continued spying for long periods of time, and, in some instances, such as in West Germany, provided the, K.G.B. not only with secrets but also with control of the intelligence apparatus itself. In the West German case, according to Bagley's analysis for the CIA, the moles were able to manipulate the careers of their fellow officers so as to promote and strategically place other K.G.B. moles. In this sense, the mole complex was self-perpetuating; and between 1960 and 1978 more than two dozen K.G.B. agents would be uncovered in the NATO alliance.

The unraveling of this complex did not occur through any ordinary security procedure but through an accident of history that could not reasonably be expected to reoccur in the intelligence war. This story began with a letter sent on April 1, 1958, to the American Ambassador in Switzerland, Henry J. Taylor. Taylor promptly turned the letter over to the CIA station chief in his embassy. Tennent Bagley, one of the CIA officers who took control of the case, recalled to me that the letter was written in fluent German, and that the author, who claimed to be a high-ranking officer of a Communist intelligence service, refused to divulge his name or even nationality. The mysterious author suggested, according to Bagley's recollection of the case, that there were moles in Western intelligence who would betray him if he identified himself. He therefore proposed helping Western intelligence put "its own house in order," presumably by ferreting out the moles, before he would consider defecting to the West. He signed the letter "Heckenschiitze."

In his initial reports, sent to mailing addresses supplied by the CIA, "Heckenschiitze" rapidly identified seven Soviet spies. These included a British admiralty aide at the Portland Naval Base, named Harry Houghton, who had been supplying the KGB with secret information about United States nuclear submarines; Col. Israel Beer, an Israeli military historian who, in fact, was an Austrian who had emigrated to Israel 20 years earlier, pretended to be an Orthodox Jew and gradually won the confidence of Prime Minister David Ben-Gurion and other Israeli leaders; and Col. Stig Wennerstrom, the Swedish air attaché in Washington, who was actually a general in the KGB.

"Heckenschiitze" also provided a document that caused serious embarrassment at the British Secret Service - a purported list of 26 Polish officials compiled by British agents in Warsaw as potential targets for recruitment. This list, "Heckenschiitze" explained, had come from the KGB When Bagley and other CIA officers evaluated the list, the question arose: How could the KGB have obtained such a sensitive document unless it had a mole inside the British Secret Service?

The British intelligence asserted that the names could have been taken out of the Warsaw telephone directory. The denials were so heated that even the usually suspicious Angleton was prepared to believe that the anonymous mole was a dispatched agent attempting to sow discord between the American and British services.

Next, to everyone's astonishment, a researcher in the CIA's Eastern European Division discovered that British intelligence had sent essentially the same list to the CIA a year or so earlier. It now became clear to the CIA officers handling the case that the list had not been lifted from the Warsaw phone book, but from the secret files of British intelligence.

Allen Dulles, then the Director of Central Intelligence, presented this evidence to his British counterpart, and, after several months of investigating those who had access to the list, British intelligence traced the probable leak to the safe of George Blake. Blake, a Dutch-born intelligence officer, had rapidly risen in the ranks of the British Secret Service through a remarkable string of successful recruitments of Communist officers in Germany. Could such successes have been purposely provided by the KGB to enhance Blake's standing?

During his interrogation, Blake admitted that he had spied for the Soviet Union since 1952 and that he had passed virtually every important document the British Secret Service had in its files to the KGB.

The depth of this KGB penetration into British intelligence stunned the CIA When the British diplomats Guy Burgess and Donald Maclean had defected to the Soviet Union in 1951, Harold (Kim) Philby, an officer in the British Secret Service, also had come under suspicion and, in the early 1950's, he had been effectively retired. The Philby case was now reopened. Then, after Blake's confession, Anthony Blunt, a former officer in the British security service (MI5), who had retired at the end of the war, was confronted by British interrogators and, in return for a grant of immunity, admitted that he had served as a Soviet mole. (In 1963, Philby defected to Moscow, thereby clearing up any doubts about his loyalties, and about his loyalties, and, then, Blake escaped from prison, and also went to Moscow.

Heckenshulttze next turned his attention to the West German intelligence service, the BND, headed by General Reinhard Gehlen, Hitler's former intelligence chief against the Russia. The BND worked closely with the CIA, which had created it.

"Heckenschiitze" reported in 1959 that he had been told by a high-ranking KGB officer that the BND had been thoroughly infiltrated by Soviet intelligence, and that many of its top officers had been blackmailed by the KGB into cooperating with it. He stated

73

that of the six BND Officers who had visited CIA head quarters in Washington in 1956. And Allen Dulles with met, two was KGB Moles. This lead was specific enough to identify immediately one member of the group, Heinz Felfe.

A former Nazi Officer, Felfe, was the deputy chief of West German counterintelligence. Like Blake, Felfe had risen to his high Position through a series of "successes." West German security Police immediately placed Felfe under close surveillance, and caught him transmitting secrets. The surveillance led to the arrest of a number of other moles in West German intelligence, including Hans Clemens, the man in charge, ironically enough, of the surveillance team in Bonn. (Felfe, after being convicted of espionage, was traded to East Germany for a group of West German spies.)

A classified 1973 review of the memoirs of General Gehlen by Angleton's deputy, Raymond Rocca, termed the Felfe case a "crushing defeat" for the BND and concluded that the West German government had been "thoroughly penetrated".

"Heckenschütze" finally decided to defect to the United States in 1960. At this point, he had served 30 months as an anonymous mole. His reason: The KGB had found out about certain documents that he had sent to the CIA. And the KGB asked his help in tracking down the leak. "Heckenschutze" now knew that there was a leak in American intelligence. On Christmas Day, he arrived with his wife at the American military mission in Berlin, and was met by a contingent Of CIA officers. He identified himself as Michael Goleniewski, the vice chairman Of Polish military intelligence. He further informed the Americans that he had hidden away a cache of documents in Warsaw.
When the CIA retrieved these documents, it found thousands of pages of polish and Soviet military bulletins containing United States military secrets that could only have come from high level sources in NATO and the United States Defense Department.

Goleniewski was given an Office in Washington, where he worked with his debriefing Officers attempting to "elaborate," as he put it, the various clues. He believed, for example, that he could pinpoint the leak in the CIA that had betrayed him. He revealed that Polish intelligence had known about a 1959 CIA plan to recruit a Polish diplomat in Switzerland.

The CIA did not pursue the lead, according to Goleniewski. They spent, he claimed, "Only a few hours" on this subject, and never brought it up again.

Before the debriefing could be completed, Goleniewski presented the CIA with still another surprise; He informed his case officers that "Goleniewski had merely been a cover name he had used in Polish intelligence. His real name was Grand Duke Aleksei Nicholaevich Romanoff. He further explained to the bewildered men from the CIA that his father, Czar Nicholas, had secretly escaped from Russia to Poland after the Bolsheviks had seized power, Goleniewski told his astonished audience that he was now heir to the Czar's fortune.

When news of these disclosures reached Richard Helms, then Deputy Director for Plans, he realized that the CIA had a potentially embarrassing Problem on its hands. Goleniewski had been the most productive agent in the entire history of the CIA, revealing more than a dozen Soviet moles; the CIA, however, could not be put in the position of supporting his wild claim to the Czar's fortune. In 1964, the CIA severed its relations with its former spy. Almost exactly one Year after Goleniewski had defected in Berlin, a KGB security Officer named Anatoli Golitsyn defected from the Soviet Embassy in Helsinki, Finland, and was taken by the CIA- to Washington, where he was turned over to Angleton for questioning.

Even though he held a relatively low rank in the KGB, he said he had attended Moscow staff meetings in which the penetration of Western intelligence services was discussed. Like Goleniewski, he suggested that the KGB had infiltrated its moles in the CIA, the British Secret Service, NATO, and French Intelligence, Indeed, much of the data that he furnished on this mole complex seemed to parallel that provided earlier by Goleniewski. Golitsyn asserted additionally, however, that the KGB had managed to place its agents in France in cabinet level positions close to de Gaulle.
This Golitsyn leads focused suspicion on the French Deputy Prime

Minister, but they were insufficient for French intelligence to take any action. Golitsyn demanded an immediate payment of $1 million for his information, and received a substantial portion of it from the CIA.

According to Philippe de Vosjoli, who had been the liaison between the CIA and French intelligence in Washington, and was brought in on the case; Golitsyn insisted that at least six French intelligence officers were Soviet moles. After Golitsyn provided clues that fit two colonels in French intelligence, both were allowed to from the service. Golitsyn further described a Plan that French intelligence had devised to spy on American nuclear-missile sites. The information that French spies collected in the United States in this operation would. According to Golitsyn, be channeled to the KGB through its moles in French intelligence. It turned out that top French officers in Paris had ordered the espionage but De Vosjoli had never been informed about it. When De Vosjoli inquired about it after learning about it from Golitsyn, he received orders from his superior's in Paris to now organize the spy networks in the United States that Golitsyn had outlined. As far as de Vosjoli was concerned, this order demonstrated that French intelligence was being controlled by KGB moles and used to collect information for the Soviet Union, not France. He protested the scheme, pointing out that France had no interest in spying on American missile sites' when his orders were not changed, he resigned from French intelligence and, after being informed that he would be assassinated if he returned to France, he went into hiding in the United States.

A large number of documents that Goleniewski had left for the CIA in the tree trunk in Warsaw contained information stolen from the NATO command. There was, for example, a top-secret June 1960, report on .intelligence objectives elaborated by the commanding staff of NATO. Goleniewski claimed that some of these documents had come from a French source who was married to a Communist, who had once been associated with the French war college.

In August 1963, French intelligence photographed a NATO official passing an attaché case full of NATO documents to a Soviet Embassy official. He was Georges Paques, a former director of studies at the war college who had been an aide to nine French ministers. During his interrogation, he confessed that he had been spying for the Soviet Union for some 20 years.

In 1968, Hermann Ludke, a rear admiral in the West German Navy and the deputy chief of logistics for the NATO command, was identified by West German security police as a KGB-SPY. Two weeks after his interrogation began, Admiral Ludke was found dead; he had been shot with a rifle. German officials declared his death an apparent suicide. The same day that Ludke was killed, Gen. Holt Wendland, the deputy director of West German intelligence, was found shot to death in his headquarters, another alleged suicide. Goleniewski claimed that he had pointed to Wendland as a key Soviet mole in West German intelligence under the code name "Organizer" as early as 196. General Wendland had been the prime target of a West German security investigation and he had undergone interrogation prior to his death. He now was presumed to have been a Soviet mole for some 22 Years, according to a CIA officer who had been privy to the investigation. Within two weeks, four other German officials, who were reported to be suspects in the Ludke-Wendland cases, died violently, all alleged suicides.

Behind a ring of three barbed-wire electrified fences at Fort Meade, Md., is the headquarters of America's most secretive intelligence service the National Security Agency (NSA.). Even though it had more employees and a larger budget than any other American intelligence service, its very existence had been classified a secret in the mid 1950s, such secrecy is considered necessary because it is responsible for protecting the security of the channels through which the leaders Of the United States Government, military forces and intelligence services communicate with one another. In most cases, the NSA designs the ciphers, encoding machines and protected lines through which the nation's most closely guarded secrets are transmitted. Any breach of this system can have disastrous consequences.

Aside from protecting the nation's secret communications, the NSA intercepts and deciphers the secrets of foreign governments. Such-signal intelligence includes intercepts of telephone and radio signals, telemetry from missiles and electrical impulses from radar and sonar. Vast quantities of information about the testing, capabilities and deployment of Soviet weaponry are derived from the NSA's electronic intelligence, or ELINT. Information about Soviet intentions comes from its code and cipher operations, which is known as Communications intelligence, or COMINT.

Despite its aura of secrecy, NSA has had multiple penetrations by Soviet intelligence. On July 22, 1963, Victor Norris Hamilton, a Syrian-born research analyst at NSA headquarters, turned up in Moscow and announced that he was defecting. He had been presumably an agent of the KGB in Moscow; he joined two other former NSA employees, Bernon F- Mitchell and William H Martin, who had defected 10 the Soviet Union three years earlier. While working as KGB moles at NSA head quarters, they had provided the Soviet Union with information about the technical capabilities and locations of the super secret sensors that the NSA had employed against it, and also with data about the NSA's codes and breaking techniques.

One day after Hamilton defected from the NSA, Jack E. Dunlap, an employee of the NSA since 1958, was found dead of carbon monoxide poisoning - an apparent suicide. One month later, when Dunlap s wife found sealed packets of Government documents in the attic of their house, it was reported that he was a Soviet agent.

Col. Thomas Fox, the chief of counterintelligence of the Defense Intelligence Agency at the time of the investigation, told me that Dunlap, a native of Bogalusa, La. had been recruited by the KGB. While employed at the NSA communications-interception base at Sinop, Turkey. He had met there Major General Garrison Coverdale the chief of staff of the NSA. General Coverdale then selected Dunlap to be his personal driver at NS headquarters at Fort Meade. General Coverdale further arranged for Dunlap to receive top-secret clearance and a position in the NSA.'s traffic-analysis division. Since the general's car had "no inspection" status, Dunlap could drive off the base with documents hidden in the car and then return without anyone knowing that the material had been removed from the base.

Moreover, Dunlap had other high-level connections in the NSA

The Carroll Report, a secret Defense Department document (part of which I received through a Freedom of Information Act request) named after Gen. Joseph F. Carroll, who was asked to investigate the case, noted that Dunlap had helped a colonel at the NSA base pilfer some "expendable items of Government property" from his office. From this incident, the report deduced, "Dunlap had already had experience in circumventing NSA procedures under relatively high level tutelage." The implication was that he had expanded his access to secret files by offering to help officer's appropriate furniture and other articles from their offices.

When General Coverdale left Fort Meade in August 1959, Dunlap was reassigned as a driver to the new NSA chief of staff, General Watlington. By continuing his chauffeuring, Dunlap retained access to the "no inspection" vehicle necessary for smuggling documents on and off the base.

The Carroll Report makes it clear that Dunlap was interrogated by NSA investigators just before he died. According to Colonel Fox, the Defense Department investigating team did not establish any connection between Dunlap and the three NSA employees who fled to Moscow. Since four KGB moles had been uncovered in the NSA. the agency found it necessary to change its secret codes, encoding machinery, security procedures and entire modus operandi.

While Dunlap was chauffeuring around the NSA chief of staff at Fort Meade, the KGB developed another mole at the pinnacle of American military intelligence Lieut. Col. William Henry Whalen, who was the intelligence advisor to the Army Chief of Staff. Since Colonel Whalen, as intelligence adviser, could demonstrate a "need to know," he had access to virtually all military planning and national intelligence estimates. In return for money, he regularly supplied secrets to his Soviet case officer over a three-year period, even after he had retired from the Army because of a physical disability. According to his subsequent indictment, the highly classified data sold to the KGB included "information pertaining to atomic weaponry, missiles, military plans for the defense of Europe, estimates of comparative military capabilities, military intelligence reports and analyses, information concerning the retaliation plans by the United States Strategic Air Command and information pertaining to troop movements. He gave away, in short, a wide range of national secrets available to the Joint Chiefs of Staff. (Pleading guilty in 1966 to charges of conspiring with a Soviet agent to divulge national defense documents, Colonel Whalen was sentenced to 15 years in prison, and served six years.)

Through the services of Dunlap and Whalen, the KGB succeeded, as Angleton put it, in "opening the window" on virtually all American intelligence-gathering activities in the Soviet bloc. Just as the CIA was able to ferret out KGB moles by tracing the documents that Goleniewski provided from Moscow to their source, the KGB could presumably trace the military intelligence reports and analyses that Whalen provided to whatever traitors existed in the Soviet intelligence apparatus. During this period, 1958 to 1963, the KGB did in fact succeed in catching the CIA's two prize moles in Moscow, Peter Popov and Oleg Penkovsky. Both were executed.

Even in the light of these past Soviet successes in penetrating the NSA and Defense Department, there was considerable resistance in the intelligence community to confronting the possibility that the KGB has used the same techniques and resources to establish new and undetected moles in American intelligence. For one thing, the search can prove damaging. If it is a failure, it will be viewed as a demoralizing witch hunt; if it is successful, it will completely undercut trust in the past work of the intelligence service. Just as the British Secret Service resisted the idea that it had been infiltrated by KGB moles even after it had received the incriminating documents from Goleniewski, the FBI elected not to pursue evidence of a mole. For example, William C. Sullivan, Assistant Director of the FBI for Domestic Intelligence until 1971, describes in his autobiography how J. Edgar Hoover, the FBI Director, refused to allow him to move against what he was convinced was a Soviet mole in the FBI's New York office. He writes that after the FBI discovered a leak, he proposed transferring, one by one, all personnel out of the suspected section. Hoover replied, "Some smart newspaperman is bound to find out that we are transferring people out of the New York office," and flatly rejected the request. The source of the leak had not been removed from the office, or further identified, when Sullivan retired. Similarly, the CIA has relied on polygraph examinations to uncover moles, even though there is no empirical evidence that they work. In 1978, for example, a 23-year-old watch officer in the CIA named William Kampiles sold to the KGB a top-secret manual explaining the technical operations of the KH-11 satellite system that is used over the Soviet Union. When the CIA investigated, it discovered that there were at least 13 other missing KH-11 manuals. Kampiles had passed all his polygraphs.

The war of the moles demonstrated that the secret services of both America and Russia could be penetrated.

[This essay was originally published in the New York Times Magazine on September 28. 1980]

II. The spy who came back from the dead

Vitaliy Sergeyevich Yurchenko was dead. The swaggering 49-year old Soviet officer, who had gone over to the CIA in 1985 and then returned three months later to the KGB, had been secretly executed by a firing squad in Moscow. Supposedly, his family was even charged for the cost of the bullets. That was the story put out by the U.S. intelligence agencies in 1986. No sooner did the "news" of his execution go out on the international wire services, then Yurchenko re-appeared in Moscow, "alive and kicking", as he put it in an interview on German television.

The relentless spy war rarely emerges in this manner in the public domain. Occasionally, a defector flashes across the public consciousness like a shooting star -- and then disappears. Inside the netherworld itself, exotic battles for information are cloaked behind three innocuous-sounding terms -- "collection," "denial." and "disinformation." "Collection" is the euphemism for stealing or intercepting secrets from another nation. This may be done through human agents who infiltrate its power structure, satellite cameras that photograph its terrain from high altitudes, antennas that intercept its signals, or remote instruments that monitor its defenses. "Denial" is the defensive term of art for hiding such data from an adversary. It can be accomplished through arresting spies, camouflaging what can be seen from the sky, and encoding messages that can be intercepted. "Disinformation," the most cunning form of countering an enemy's search for secrets, is based on supplying him with data that will confuse and mislead. Rather than arresting enemy's spies and other collectors , they are purposefully fed misleading data. Such counterintelligence requires that enemy intelligence services remain in a continual sort of dance with each other, each dangling in front of the others' eyes agents who pretend to be traitors.

Yurchenko had been involved in this game when he first came to Washington in 1975. Officially, he was the security officer at the Soviet Embassy. Actually, as described in his CIA biography, he was a KGB expert on "Dangles" or "the insertion ... of agents into western, and especially American, intelligence services." These "dangles" were usually Soviet diplomats who, under KGB orders, contact western agents to misinform them. It was a cat and mouse exchange that brought this master dangler into close collaboration with the CIA. Eventually, he even allowed it to believe he himself had been recruited. In the decade in between, he provided a thread that ran through some of the West's most dramatic losses.

At the heart of the crises was the loss of one of the most valuable agents the CIA had ever acquired in the Soviet Union. He was A.G. Tolkachev, an electronics experts employed by an elite Soviet think tank that researched problems of military aviation and space detection systems. He had been recruited for the CIA in Moscow in the early 1980s, through a third-party. Unlike most other western intelligence sources -- diplomats, attaches or intelligence operatives, whose access to technology was limited, Tolkachev was in a position to pass on to the CIA technical data on the state of the art of Soviet ground and spaced-based radar, which, in turn, revealed the extent to which American submarines and planes were vulnerable to detection. For some three years, up until that spring, microfilms of these Soviet military secrets were left for an American courier in Moscow in "dead drops." Such hiding places made any face-to-face contact unnecessary.
The Tolkachev "take" was treated with the utmost security. From the CIA's station in the American Embassy, it was hand-carried to Washington. In late spring, however, the deliveries from Tolkachev abruptly ended. When the American courier, who had diplomatic immunity, went to check the "dead drop," he walked into a trap. He was seized by waiting KGB officers, who photographed the spy

paraphernalia from the dead drop, then expelled from the Soviet Union. It was now clear to the CIA that despite all its precautions, Tolkachev had been compromised and captured by the KGB.

In the spy war, the question of how an agent is compromised can be important as the loss itself. In this case, which was extremely tightly-supervised, there were only two possibilities: either Tolkachev, through some slip on his part (or his courier's) had been caught by the KGB through routine police work; or he had been betrayed to the KGB by someone inside the CIA who was privy to this ultra-secret operation. If it was the former, and his capture was due to some sort of KGB surveillance, the entire affair could be chalked up to a tragic accident. But if it was the latter, and it turned out Tolkachev had been compromised by a traitor in the CIA, all the CIA's other agents in the Soviet sphere would be in extreme jeopardy. Indeed, if this mole was strategically enough positioned, the CIA itself would be shown to be the KGB's plaything.

This possibility, as former CIA Director Richard M. Helms put it, "is the nightmare of every CIA Director." Such a "penetration," as it is called in the spy world, would not only serve to paralyze ongoing operations, it would call into question the validity of the information the CIA had already received from sources that it had believed secure but which in fact might have been compromised long ago.

This nightmare seemed more and more reality as one after another western spies came out of the cold, claiming that they had been compromised -- and were on the verge of being arrested by the KGB. First, in India, Igor Gheja, the third secretary of the Soviet Embassy, whom the CIA was secretly developing as a potential mole, defected from his post in March. He suggested that the KGB had become inexplicably suspicious of him. Under these circumstances, the United States granted him asylum.

Next, in Greece, Sergei Bokhan, a Soviet military intelligence officer, who had provided the CIA with valuable insights into Soviet efforts to infiltrate the Greek military, sought protection at the American Embassy in May. He claimed that the KGB had placed him under surveillance. His fears of imminent arrests indeed were so high that he left his wife and seven year old daughter behind. The issue was again whether their detection, as well as that of the CIA's spy in Moscow, had been caused by a leak within the CIA.

And in England, came the compromise of Oleg Antonovich Gordievsky. Gordievsky was according to the diplomatic roster the political counselor at the Soviet Embassy in London; actually he was the acting resident for the KGB-- the man in charge of its operations in England. That was only half of the picture. In this bewildering world of mirrors, Gordievsky not only was a KGB case officer administrating much of Soviet espionage conducted out of the embassies in these NATO countries, but a British double-agent, in a position to reveal the targets of Soviet operations to Western intelligence. He had been recruited by MI-6 in Copenhagen, and then had been carefully groomed over the years as a mole.

Just as the CIA's agent Tolkachev was compromised in Moscow, Gordievsky's secret liaison with MI-6 was unraveled by the KGB. While preparing to go to Moscow for his summer leave, he realized the KGB was on to him, and hastily organized his escape (abandoning his wife and two children in the process). Telling his British case officers he was about to be arrested, he asked for asylum, and his defection was hastily arranged.

Although British intelligence attempted to put the best face on its loss by expelling the usual suspects among Soviet diplomats, trade officials and correspondents in England, it was an intelligence disaster. It ended a long and expensive MI-6 operation that had begun years earlier, when he was a lowly press attaché at the Soviet Embassy in Denmark. (The exact period of his service as a British mole is a carefully guarded secret, protected by a bodyguard of lies, purposely leaked by officials. As one former counter-intelligence officer explained, in response to published accounts that Gordievsky had been recruited 15 years ago, "The last thing an intelligence service tells its adversary is an honest date.") MI-6 reportedly had indeed helped advance his career in the KGB, as far as was practical, by giving him bits of information -- "chickenfeed," as it is called -- to make him appear more successful. These efforts apparently came to fruition in 1985 when he was promoted, after the British expelled his boss, Yuri Gok, to the position of acting KGB resident in London. The final coup for British intelligence would have been keeping him in this position so that he could identify all unknown and new KGB recruitments of British citizens. When instead his cover was blown, he was forced to escape. The fact that in the months following his defection not a single British citizen with access to state secrets was apprehended suggests that, if the KGB had its share of moles in England, he may not have had the time, or access, to learn their identity. (The Soviet diplomats who were expelled would have been known in any case to MI-5 through surveillance).

While these defections could be trumpeted from a public relations perspective as "victories," which had been secretly won long ago and could now be revealed, they constituted a defeat in the ongoing spy war, since they diminished the capacity to get secret. Spies are most valuable as sources of when they are in the enemy camp. They then, and only then, have access to its vital secrets. Moreover, they can remove the secrets in such a way that they are not missed. Documents, for example, are not themselves stolen; they are microfilmed or copied, so that the enemy does not learn that they have been compromised. The moment, however, a spy actually defects to the West, he negates his past value. Not only does he lose his access to enemy secrets, but he exposes the fact that he has stolen secrets in the past -- which often allows at least part of the damage to be remedied. In the case of Gordievsky, for example, British intelligence not only lost a mole in place, all the previous secrets he revealed would now be known to the KGB -- and, where possible, remedied.

This rapid succession of losses in far flung parts of the world had to be explained: Did the KGB have inside information? Just as the CIA was investigating this ugly -- and divisive issue, it received an astonishing message from Moscow. It was from the dangle man, Yurchenko.

The last time Yurchenko had been actually seen in Washington was the summer of 1980, when he was re-assigned to Moscow. Before he left for Russia, the CIA also made its own approach to him, offering him an opportunity to himself become a doble-agent for the CIA. It was the sort of a gambit that is commonly made by the

CIA on the remote chance that a KGB officer at some future time will run into difficulties that will cause him to accept. That was the last time he was heard from until this unexpected contact.

Now he informed the CIA that, since leaving Washington, he had a meteoric rise in the KGB and was a General - designate in KGB headquarters at Dzerzhinskii Square. He explained that on his return to Moscow he had been assigned to the First Chief Directorate, which had the responsibility for gathering foreign intelligence. Because of his successes, he had been promoted to the chief of the Fifth counterintelligence department. Here he was responsible for, among other things, investigating, the credentials of foreign agents recruited by the KGB -- a job which involved using "special drugs" on occasion. He also said he had the task of investigating suspected cases of treason among KGB personnel. Moreover, in April 1985, he was again elevated to being deputy chief of the department specifically responsible for organizing espionage operations against the United States -- which included not only supervising Soviet agents but coordination their efforts with those from other Eastern bloc countries. He was, if this incredible self-reported career was authentic, not only the higest-ranking KGB officer ever to volunteer his services to the West, but a man uniquely qualified to definitively answer the questions that had plagued American intelligence for over a decade and, more specifically, the burning ones that had just arisen. As the investigator of treason, he could explain how the KGB had managed to capture Tolkachev -- and zero in on Gordievsky and the other western intelligence spies that spring; as deputy chief of the First Directorate, he could give way the Communist bloc apparatus in North America for recruiting and servicing its agents; and, most important, as the counterintelligence executive responsible for "vetting" the foreign recruits by the KGB, he could identify any and all moles that had been infiltrated into American intelligence.

Although his motive was still unclear, General-designate Yurchenko indicated that he prepared to resolve all these crucial issues for the CIA by divulging the KGB's most closely-guarded secrets: the sources and methods it used. To this end, he offered to rendezvous with CIA case officers in Rome the last week in July.

The initial interrogation took place in a safe house on the outskirts of the city. Yurchenko then told the CIA a message that it had desperately wanted to believe: All the attempted recruitments of CIA personnel, which came under his purview, had failed. There was no mole in the CIA. He could personally attest to that.

Instead of moles, he explained that the KGB had used exotic means of surveillance to uncover Soviet agents in contact with western intelligence. The most effective of these techniques he claimed was a telltale spy dust, which was sprayed on American diplomats in Moscow suspected of being couriers. They would then unwittingly get this dust on whatever they touched including clandestine letters, which could then be detected by machines in the central post office, and traced to the recipient. In addition, he also suggested that the KGB had made use of information it received from a former American intelligence officer's code-named "Robert."

Yurchenko had another surprise. Rather than returning to Moscow, as had been expected, he announced that wanted to defect to the United States. He also expected to be paid handsomely for his future discloses.

The KGB general-designate thus began his curious odyssey. On August 1st, he applied for political asylum at the US embassy in Rome. The next day he was bundled aboard a military courier plane, and flown to the United States. Officially, he entered the United States on CIA parole.

Once ensconced in safe house, he began his debriefings. Questioned more intensely about the mystery agent "Robert," he explained that the ex-CIA officer had visited the Soviet Embassy in Washington in 1983, and subsequently he had traveled to St. Anton, Austria for a meeting with the KGB. These details immediately focused suspicion on an ex-CIA employee who had been previously spotted by FBI surveillance at the Soviet Embassy in 1983 -- Edward Lee Howard.

Howard had joined the CIA in 1981 at the age of 29. He was groomed over the next two years for an embassy job in Moscow. Before undertaking the assignment, however, he made damaging admission about drug-taking during his lie detector examination.

After his career ended at the CIA, in June 1983, he made a telephone call to a Soviet diplomat, hanging up without speaking; and then he walked by the gates of the Soviet Embassy several times -- as if he was trying to make contact. This suspicious activity exposed him to surveillance by the FBI, which routinely maintains around the clock surveillance on the Soviet Embassy with a large team of "watchers" and "listeners." When he was subsequently questioned by the CIA's Office of Security, he admitted that he had gone to the Soviet Embassy with the idea of giving them secrets, but denied he had made contact. Whether or not this latter assertion was true, it certainly provided fair warning that he might make future contacts with the KGB, which he did in Austria the following year.

Howard eventually moved back to Santa Fe where he got a job as an economic analyst for the state of New Mexico. After Yurchenko's pointing to "Robert." The FBI questioned him, and he freely acknowledged that he had met with Soviet officials in St Anton, Austria. Since the date of the meeting coincided with the one Yurchenko described, it was clear that he was "Robert."

The real issue was not whether Howard had contacted the Soviets, but whether he was in a position to have betrayed Tolkachev. When Howard left the CIA in 1983 he was hardly more than a trainee and not privy to the CIA's closely-held "need to know" secrets, such as the identity of its top agent. It was, however, always possible, that he could have picked up some telltale clue which would have, two years later, pointed to Tolkachev. Before this crucial question could be resolved, Howard disappeared from his house in Santa Fe, under the very eyes of the FBI agents watching the house. He boarded a commercial flight to Austin, Texas. There the trail ended-- until he resurfaced in Moscow in 1986.

Yurchenko also furnished leads pointing directly to Ronald W. Pelton -- an ex-employee of the National Security Agency, a super secret code-breaking unit, which is the US equivalent of the British GSCC. Five years earlier, on January 15 1980, Pelton had spoken to Yurchenko at the Soviet Embassy in Washington D.C., and then met there and in Austria with other Soviet intelligence officers. Pelton had been an incredible catch for the KGB. He had served at the N.S.A. as a specialist in interception equipment used to eavesdrop on, and record, Soviet underwater communications, and, in this capacity, had access to one of America's most tightly-sealed "compartments" -- intelligence-gathering operations involving submarines planting listening devices in Soviet waters. Yurchenko would have been fully aware of the value of Pelton's secrets: He had himself coincidentally worked at an earlier point in his career on Soviet countermeasures to US submarine detection through exotic surveillance.

In both cases, however, Yurchenko had only told U.S. intelligence what he, and Soviet intelligence, could presume it already knew. As the security officer at the Soviet Embassy in 1980, Yurchenko certainly was aware that Soviet telephone lines were tapped by the FBI, and that visitors photographed by the FBI. In both cases, it could be presumed that had been picked up by FBI surveillance in 1980. In Pelton's case, The FBI had indeed received advanced warning of the visit -- twice -- when Pelton had called the Embassy to arrange the meeting. Moreover, as the Soviets knew from the conversation, he had effectively identified himself over the tapped line as a U.S. Government employee with information to give. From its photography and visual surveillance, the FBI could further determine his general physical characteristics -- white, mustached, middle-age and male. With these clues, it would only be a matter of checking through the few hundred photographs of recently-discharged men that fit this description before the FBI would across Pelton, who had left the NSA in July 1979. The KGB could presume alarm bells would be set off when the by his classified status. Further, even if it had not assumed that Pelton had been compromised from the beginning -- or tracked down soon afterwards by the FBI -- the fact that he had failed to show up at a schedule meeting in Vienna in April 1985 would have suggested that, if not caught, he had little further value to the KGB. In the case of Edward Howard, the KGB could have learned from Howard himself during its long interrogation of him that he had been detected, questioned and made a limited admission to the CIA's Office of Security before he actually met with Soviet intelligence officers. He was, in any eventuality, a burned-out case since 1983 -- caught by FBI surveillance, fired from the CIA and he had no further access to secrets. Whatever the value of Yurchenko's redundant tips, the CIA decided to play these "revelations" as a trump card in its relations with Congress.

In this context, John McMahon, then the CIA's Deputy Director, paid an extraordinary visit to the office of Senator Malcolm Wallop (Republican, Wyoming) On October 31st 1985 -- the eve of Halloween. McMahon, who had headed the clandestine side of the CIA in the previous administration, had found himself the target of the influential Senator's criticism. Indeed, that evening Senator Wallop began by recalling to him that his visit coincided with the sixth anniversary of the CIA's Halloween Massacre -- a wholesale computerized purge of its Directorate of Operations, which was responsible for gathering and analyzing secret intelligence.

The Deputy Director responded, knowing he held trump, by asking him why he assumed these re-organizations had an effect on operations. Wallop explained that his concern was that the CIA's function of evaluating and testing intelligence had been so seriously degraded by these "purges" that the CIA was no longer conceptually capable of recognizing disinformation planted among its Soviet sources.

McMahon replied that the CIA had acquired a source, so high up in the KGB, that he could assure Senator Wallop that his concern was ill-founded. As Wallop listened in amazement, he sprung Yurchenko on him. He explained that this former deputy head of the KGB's key espionage unit had already provided the United States with an unprecedented insight into the spy war.
Yurchenko's revelation that KGB had acquired all its secrets about the CIA from a few ex-officers, such as Howard and Pelton -- put to rest the long and debilitating debate about moles in the CIA. According to him, the KGB had failed during the past five years to recruit a single active CIA officer. If it had, he insisted he would have known it. Even more reassuring to the CIA, Yurchenko claimed that the KGB had not managed to dupe the CIA with "dangles" -- or false defectors.

This was the startling conclusion that McMahon presented to Senator Wallop. As far as he was concerned, Yurchenko's revelations demonstrated that his long-standing concern over the penetration of the CIA was unfounded. And that the CIA had more than able to deal with the KGB.

Although McMahon's purpose in this Halloween visit was to end any lingering doubts this influential Senator might have about the CIA, Senator Wallop was still not entirely satisfied. He asked McMahon whether the CIA had considered any "alternative hypotheses" about Yurchenko, or the information he had provided. Was it possible, for example that Yurchenko had been sent over by the KGB to misinform the CIA by telling it what it- wanted to hear? Was his purpose in giving away inactive agents, who no longer had any value to the KGB, such as Pelton and Howard, to divert attention away from still active KGB agents in American intelligence? Was he really who he said he was in the KGB or might the career he reported to the CIA be nothing more than a legend designed to enhance his credibility? And indeed he held the position of "deputy head" in the KGB, why had he not provided the CIA with the complete list of the KGB's illegal assets -- i.e. or the agents it had who were not under diplomatic cover in North America?

McMahon responded that no other hypothesis was necessary. He acknowledged that Yurchenko had not yet provided the CIA with the KGB's "wiring diagram," as the illegal network is termed, but expected that would be elicited from him in the near future. As for the information Yurchenko had provided, not only had it checked out, but it was, as he put it, "dynamite." Among other things, the deputy director explained that he had provided a list of western journalists in Moscow whom the KGB considered "trusted contacts" -- and he had identified two traitors' in U.S. intelligence. As far as John McMahon was concerned, this was absolute proof that Yurchenko was who he claimed to be -- a high-ranking KGB executive, which had changed over to the American side. He then dramatically concluded his presentation by saying, "I would stake my career on Yurchenko's bona fides." It was a statement that he would have cause to regret in 48 hours.

While the CIA's deputy director sung his praises, Yurchenko actually was silently biding his time in an isolated two story house, surrounded by woods and a lake, some 22 miles outside of Washington. He had become, after delivering his initial messages, progressively less forthcoming. Instead of revealing the much sought after KGB "wiring diagram" of illegal spies, as McMahon had suggested, Yurchenko was stonewalling questions about it. Moreover, his repeatedly claim that the KGB had made no other recruits in the United States or Canada during the five years that he was in charge of the KGB's counterintelligence unit was becoming increasingly less credible. His CIA case officer, who was a veteran of the Soviet Bloc division, determined that the Soviet Union had accepted recruits during this period both in Canada and the United States. The CIA, after all, had sent its own "dangles" to the KGB during this period: both to pass disinformation and test its procedures. These included American diplomats, military attaches and intelligence officers who feigned disloyalty to the United States. Since these double-agents would all be known to and vetted by Yurchenko, if he indeed held the position he claimed, his failure to name them -- even when led in their direction by his case officer -- raised very serious questions about his authenticity as a defector.

Moreover, aside from these American dangles, he claimed total ignorance about the existence of dozens of elaborate hiding places for messages that Soviet illegals had prepared for spies. This was all part of the "wiring diagram" that Yurchenko, as the KGB's section deputy chief for North America, should have known like the back of his hand. The more he was pressed, the more recalcitrant he became. Even the offer of a million dollar contract, in which he would collect generous bounties for each Soviet mole he identified, failed to move him to reveal KGB operations. For the most part during these debriefings, he merely repeated what the CIA already knew from other sources. It was even questionable whether his disclosures about Pelton and Howard had done little more than identified Soviet sources that had long ago been spotted by FBI surveillance -- but not arrested because it was judged that the damage of such a move would outweigh the benefits. This indeed was indicated by President Reagan himself, who stated, in regard to Yurchenko, "The information he provided was not anything new or sensational."

There were also evident parallels with an earlier defector that had nearly wrecked the CIA's Soviet Bloc Division. He was Yuri Nosenko, a KGB officer, who, after playing games with the CIA for two years, defected in Switzerland in 1964. Like Yurchenko, Nosenko claimed to work in KGB headquarters in Moscow -- a position, in both cases, which the CIA no independent way of verifying. These two defectors were in fact the only ones ever to come from this inner sanctum. And like Yurchenko, Nosenko came with a message that implied that there was no mole, or other serious leak, in the CIA. Instead, he also cited chemical "spy dusts" to explain how the KGB had uncovered an important CIA agent in Russia. As far as human sources went, Nosenko, like Yurchenko, identified only retired and burned-out American agents, who, in any case, no longer had access to secrets.

Despite these similarities, there was a crucial difference in the way the two defectors were treated. Soon after Nosenko arrived in the United States, the head of the Soviet Bloc Division, concerned that the KGB officer might "redefect" to facilitate, as he put in a 1964 memorandum, "a massive propaganda assault on the CIA," ordered him imprisoned in escape-proof quarters.« This was not a mistake that the Soviet Bloc Division was about to repeat in the case of Yurchenko.

In September, Yurchenko asked to see a Soviet acquaintance in Canada -- the wife of high-ranking Soviet diplomat in Montreal; with whom he represented he was having a romantic liaison. The CIA accommodated this request, and even took him to Canada for a meeting with her. (Ordinarily, according to former counterintelligence officers, KGB defectors on parole are prohibited from contacting Soviet citizens -- both for their own safety and to prevent them from giving any signals to former comrades. Afterwards, there were few, if any more, interrogation sessions for Yurchenko. The game finally drew to an end on November 2nd -- exactly three months to the day after his arrival in America -- a cold rainy Saturday afternoon. If the CIA did not actually return its parolee to the Soviet Embassy, his case officers certainly facilitated it. First, they took him to a clothing store in the nearby town of Manassas, and bought him a coat, hat and umbrella. They also gave him the opportunity to make two long-distance calls to the Soviet Embassy, and in one he advised the officer on duty he was returning. Then, he was handed over to a lone CIA officer who drove him to a convenient restaurant a few blocks from the Soviet Embassy compound. At this point, he indicating to him that he was free to go, and watched as Yurchenko walked out the door, and put on his new coat and hat. After he was gone, his CIA companion called neither the FBI or Washington police, who could have intercepted him at the gates of the embassy compound. Yurchenko later telephoned a CIA phone number he had been given to advise that he had safely arrived at his destination. Whatever else it was, it could hardly be called an escape.

The affair might have ended then and there if Yurchenko had quietly returned to Moscow on his diplomatic passport. Even if anyone asked about him, the CIA was under no obligation to respond to queries about double-agents.

The KGB, however, had yet another surprise in store for the CIA, and its deputy director, who had already bet his reputation on Yurchenko. That Monday, November 4th, reporters received an invitation to a televised news conference that afternoon. The star was none other than Yurchenko (who, as far as was publicly known, was still the CIA's prize defector.)

Mocking the CIA at every opportunity, Yurchenko egregiously claimed that he had been kidnapped from Rome, drugged and held a prisoner for three months by the CIA. It was not a story that was true or even meant to be believed.

Earlier that week, the State Department had lodged a protest with the Soviet Foreign Ministry charging that in 1977 an American intelligence agent, named Nicholas Shadrin, had been paralyzed with drugs by the KGB in Vienna, and transported across international borders to Hungary, where he died. The source for this assertion, as released to the press, supposedly was Yurchenko. Now, the Soviet Embassy filed an almost identical protest with the State Department, charging one of its officials, Yurchenko, had been paralyzed with drugs by the CIA, and taken across international borders. The source for this story was also Yurchenko. A single KGB officer thus had the distinction, in a five day period, of being the source for both American and Soviet protests; both of which were also denied.

The next day he went to the State Department to demonstrate that he was acting without Soviet coercion. He met there with a half dozen CIA and State Department officials -- as well as a psychologist -- who agreed, after nearly a half hour session with him, that he was returning voluntarily to the Soviet Union. As he left, he jauntily clasped his hands over his head as a victory sign. By Wednesday, the Soviet dangle man was on an Aeroflot plane heading home -- his mission completed.

As this amazing case unraveled before his eyes, Senator Patrick J. Leahy, the vice chairman of the intelligence committee, concluded that Yurchenko was a double agent who the KGB "foisted" on the CIA "This whole thing was very good theater," the President's National Security Advisor told the New York Times, "And, to me, theater is something that is staged." There were indeed two prudent reasons for such a conclusion. Yurchenko trusted the KGB sufficiently to return to its fold; and the KGB trusted Yurchenko enough to permit him to return two days later to the State Department.

The Soviet Union has no history of granting amnesty to, or otherwise forgiving, intelligence officers who betray state secrets. Pointedly, the acronym for its counterespionage arm, SMERSH, stood for its slogan, "Death to All Traitors." As a 25 year old veteran of KGB counterespionage, Yurchenko certainly knew the fate that would have awaited a traitor -- or any KGB officer that had, without proper authority, divulging secret data to the CIA. While there are many cases of ordinary Soviet citizens, and even ballet dancers, intellectuals, journalists and soldiers -- who did not have access to state secrets -- returning to the Soviet Union without facing punishment, KGB officers, who commit treason, fall into a different category. For that reason, any Soviet intelligence officers who returned to Russia, without punishment for his putative treason, was presumed by the CIA to have been acting under KGB orders in feigning disloyalty. In fact, there had never been a previous case -- in least in the public record -- of a KGB officer who, after defecting to the United States, re-defecting.)
Yurchenko's voluntary return could be explained in two ways. Either he had not been a traitor but a KGB officer sent on a mission; or he had been a traitor and he was acting completely irrationally in putting himself in the hands of the KGB -- even though it meant facing death or imprisonment.
The possibility that Yurchenko was crazed, irrational or even unstable on November 4th does not satisfactorily explain, however,

the Soviet Embassy's next move in the drama-- its decision to send Yurchenko back to the State Department for an interview where he would be examined by CIA representatives, psychologists and state Department officials. At any point during this interview, he could again offer to defect. If he had been upset at the handling of his case by the CIA, or disturbed by the threat of unanticipated Soviet reprisals against himself or his family, the CIA could conceivably find some way of reassuring him. If he had indeed been a traitor who had changed his mind, he could, at least from the Soviet perspective, change it again under American persuasion. The Soviet embassy could have kept Yurchenko in its confines indefinitely. It was under no obligation to place him back into American hands on November 6th, and give him another opportunity to save his life by defecting again. Such a risk would be inconceivable if Yurchenko had actually been a traitor, and divulged secrets from KGB headquarters for three months because Soviet intelligence would need to exhaustively determine from him in precise detail every iota of information he revealed -- or even knew. This kind of damage assessment would require intense interrogation of Yurchenko, by experts familiar with the cases in which he had been involved for a quarter of a century. This meant that the KGB would now have to keep tight control over him -- until he was squeezed of every drop of information.

Under this circumstance, Yurchenko would not have been returned to America officials if he was unstable, deranged or untrustworthy. The KGB could hardly trust a traitor, especially one who changed sides irrationally. Indeed, it could only be fully confident that he would return from the State Department if it knew Yurchenko was a well-disciplined KGB officer who had already proven himself loyal by carrying out his provocative assignment. The fact that he was allowed to go to the State Department, and to give a press conferences in Washington D.C., showed that the Soviets had full confidence in his rationality.

After Yurchenko returned to the KGB in Moscow -- where he added insult to injury by holding yet another press conference -- the CIA acted to submerge the spy war from public sight. It simply declared that Yurchenko had been a "bona fide" defector -- a term used by the CIA when a defector demonstrates his good faith and loyalty to the United States by his subsequent actions. In previous cases, it took defectors years to earn them. In this case, Yurchenko had betrayed U.S. intelligence by returning to Moscow and divulging, publicly and presumably privately, secret details of his CIA debriefing. Never before had a defector earned his "bona fides" in such a perverse manner.

The end play of this double sting had shattering implications for the CIA. Not only had its deputy director tied his own credibility to the validity of this temporary defector, but the Director of the CIA, William Casey, also pronounced him to be "real" prior to his embarrassing return. Far more important, his re-defection threatened to rekindle the entire issue of whether or not the KGB had been duping American intelligence. The re-defection also left unresolved the mystery of the betrayal of the American agent in Moscow. If Yurchenko was nothing more than a double-agent, dangled by the KGB in Rome and then reeled back again in Washington, it had then to be assumed that the message he delivered also came from the KGB and, even if factually accurate, it was a red herring, designed to confuse its investigation of the betrayal. He had pointed investigators in the direction of a new Soviet surveillance device, the so-called spy dust, and a "spent" ex-CIA employee. If this was the wrong trail, it meant that the KGB had other means of learning the identity of western agents, and it was going to great lengths to protect it. The search for an active mole in the CIA, threatened to again pry open a Pandora's Box of suspicions and troubles.

[This Essay was originally published in Life in September 1986]

III. The Ames Postscript

Aldrich Ames arrest as an alleged Soviet mole in the CIA raises serious question about both the CIA's past and future as an espionage services. "Think of an espionage service as a highly specialized employment service," explained James Jesus Angleton, the former chief of counterintelligence. Such recruiters aim to find foreign government officials with legitimate access to secret documents. Up to a point, like more conventional corporate headhunters, they consults biographical files to find a candidate to fill an opening, observe his work (or even interview him) and make him an offer to change his loyalties that will have difficulty refusing. But unlike their counterparts in the private sector, these recruiters do not ask the candidates to give up their old jobs. Instead, they insist he maintain two positions simultaneously: one for his own government and one for his new and secret employer. If the recruit does not have access to needed material, his secret employer takes on the task of managing his career by providing him with "successes" in the form of cases and information, so he rises to where he is useful. As the CIA's Soviet bloc division noted in 1973 about its own capabilities at career-managing a potential mole recruited at a foreign embassy: "we are prepared to guide and assist him in his career, running him in place until he develops the access we need."

Yet while CIA officials have the utmost confidence in their ability to successfully mount such grand plots against Russia, many of these same officials are unable to accept that the KGB has a similar capacity for conspiracy. (Former CIA Director Colby said, for instance "I thought the function of the agency was to penetrate the Kremlin not protect itself against the KGB.") These officials placed great faith in the CIA's lie detector tests and other routine security procedures and derided those who had less faith in these defenses -- notably Angleton and his counterintelligence staff -- as "paranoid," indulging in "sick think" or otherwise out of touch with reality. The Ames case demonstrates that such faith was misplaced.

The KGB clearly had the ability to compromise, recruit, career-manage, service and utilize the intelligence product of Ames for an extensive period of time. According to the FBI affidavits, Ames had been in illicit liaison with the Soviet intelligence service since at least 1984 -- and, according to a former CIA counterintelligence executive, he may have been recruited much earlier. Moreover, he had been, while a Soviet mole, head of the CIA's Soviet counterintelligence unit. From this vantage point Ames could vet the secret information coming in to the CIA from its own spies in Russia and tell the KGB what the CIA was learning.

The implications of this case are far reaching. To begin with, it casts new light on the intellectual provenance of the information supplied to the media by retired KGB officers. For example,

Oleg Kalugin, who served as a Major General in the KGB up until 1987, was certainly in a position to know of the KGB's success in penetrating the CIA. Yet, he stated categorically in 1992: "No responsible politician or government employee was ever recruited by the Soviets in Europe or America in the last 20 years." Kalugin added that the KGB had so little hard currency at its disposal that, to pay operating expenses abroad, it had to open up "its archives to the foreign media" and sell documents. While this picture of KGB ineptitude and poverty may have come as welcome news inside the CIA, it hardly squared with the millions the KGB was then paying to Ames to get leverage over CIA counterintelligence.

More important, Ames' work for the KGB calls into serious question the validity of the secret intelligence derived from Russia in the mid and late 1980s. Ames is said to have identified to the KGB the 10 CIA agents in the Soviet Union which were supplying the CIA with data. Yet, just as a Mafia suspect who found out some of his phones were tapped by police could use them to mislead the police, the KGB, following the usual practice in counterintelligence, would not immediately arrest the 10 sources Ames told them about but use them to pass misleading information to the CIA. If it controlled all the CIA's sources through Ames, it could assure that each reports persuasively dove-tailed with the others. This might explain why the CIA was egregiously wrong in assessing various Soviet capabilities in the mid 1980s.

The Ames revelation also helps to understand some pivotal KGB activities of the 1980s. Consider, for example, the short-lived visit of Vitaliy Yurchenko to Washington in August 1985. He claimed to be a KGB defector, and Ames, as the relevant CIA counterintelligence officer, was assigned to the debriefing team. Yurchenko identified himself as the deputy chief of the KGB unit specifically responsible for organizing and supervising its espionage against the United States, which conveniently put him in a perfect position to identify KGB recruits in the CIA. Thus the head of the debriefing team immediately asked him whether or not there were any KGB moles presently working in the CIA and offered him, as is the practice, a substantial bonus if he provides any information that could help locate such a mole. Since Ames was already a mole, Yurchenko, if he were a genuine defector, had a truly golden opportunity.

But instead of naming Ames, he insisted falsely (like Kalugin later did) that the KGB had not succeeded in making a single recruit of any CIA officer on active duty. (On the contrary, he diverted attention away from Ames by identifying a former employee of the CIA, Edward Lee Howard who had contacted the Soviet Embassy, as both the FBI and CIA had already determined from its routine surveillance.) After 90 days as a temporary defector -- during which period, he helped Ames, who was checking out his story, expand his access, Yurchenko redefected back to Moscow.

Finally, the most serious ramification of the Ames case is the indication that Ames might not have been alone. As one top former CIA counterintelligence officer put it, "moles, like mice, are not often found as singletons." Ames, who had access to counterintelligence files, would be in a position to provide the KGB with a roster of candidates. The ex-CIA officer recalled that in similar mole operations into the intelligence services of West Germany, England and France, the KGB had acted to widen the original penetration by having the initial recruit spot, assess and find the vulnerability of others in the service for its head-hunters. It is assumed that Ames did the same. Moreover, the fact that Ames managed to rise to be head of the CIA's Soviet counterintelligence unit despite his reportedly lackluster performance and, at the same time, avoid all the CIA's security defenses, suggests that he might have had inside "career management" help. This possibility is reinforced by the chronology of the payments Ames received from the KGB, as detailed in the FBI affidavits. These payments extended six years after he had been transferred out of the counterintelligence unit to Rome, the UN in New York and the CIA's boon dock anti- narcotics unit, where his "need to know" access would be greatly curtailed. In the words of the ex-CIA counterintelligence officer: "the KGB does not pay bonuses of such magnitude on spec." So it appears Ames was able to deliver secrets on the Soviet's shopping list from areas in which he did not have access. If so, he must have relied on others. For the last two decades, the CIA hoped it could evade this nightmare of moles by such mechanistic means as lie-detect examinations. Now, that the KGB succeeded in its conspiratorial enterprise, the CIA again has to confront the issue of protecting itself.

[This essay was published in the Wall Street Journal on March 8, 1994]

IV. The Bagley Reprise

On February 18 2014, the very day he died, Tennent Peter Bagley, a former deputy head of the CIA's Soviet Russia Division, sent me a 35-page memorandum summing up his thoughts on cases that had bedeviled the CIA for five decades. His view on the Top Hat case is excerpted below.

The affair called "Tophat" may be the most complex and least understood of all the spy episodes of the Cold War. CIA insiders have called it their greatest spying success against the Soviet Union -- which it may have been -- but unbeknownst to them, the KGB's hand had lain behind it. An extraordinary twist had transformed it from KGB provocation to CIA triumph. The Soviet unit that launched the operation -- the KGB's internal-security directorate (Second Chief Directorate -- SCD) kept it so secret that they allowed only two people in the KGB's entire foreign-intelligence directorate (First Chief Directorate -- FCD) to know even of its existence. As a result, even today, a quarter century after the Cold War and a half century after it began, the story remains only partly known -- East or West -- and no one can answer with authority all the questions it left hanging.

Among the unknowns lurks a KGB mole inside CIA. The first breach in the wall of security surrounding this case came long after the end of the Cold War, from one of those two KGB foreign-directorate higher-ups who knew.

Thanks to him we can now see that the "Tophat" story really began long before GRU Colonel Dmitry Polyakov contacted American Intelligence, not then in late 1961 but almost five years earlier, at that shocking moment in 1957 when the KGB learned (from a mole inside CIA) that a traitor was stripping the country's military secrets. So damaging was this leak, so widespread its political and strategic implications, that the investigation was taken over by the chief of Soviet counterintelligence himself -- KGB General Oleg Gribanov, "the Soviet J. Edgar Hoover."

In mid-November 1958 he had GRU Lieutenant Colonel Pyotr S. Popov recalled on a ruse from his post in East Berlin, arrested and interrogated. Popov confessed. For six years he had been passing to CIA secrets of Soviet weapons developments and tactics for atomic warfare. In addition he had opened up his service to the CIA: the GRU's procedures, some of its spies abroad, and hundreds of its officers. The GRU chief General Mikhail A. Shalin was fired, and in early December the KGB chief Ivan Serov himself moved over to replace him and straighten things out.

But to Oleg Gribanov this shattering of the GRU looked more like opportunity than disaster. Long experience had taught his organization that in counterintelligence work, "he who takes the initiative, all other things being equal, achieves the best results." Not to wait passively to detect spies but to go out aggressively to find them (or make them.) Working on this principle the KGB had formed or taken over organizations of resistance to their own regime, and used them to expose and mislead their opponents inside the country and abroad; to lead hostile intelligence services down false paths, and to compromise and recruit their personnel as moles. So successful had they been that some of these operations like "Trust" and "Sindikat-2" of the 1920s became celebrated in Soviet history, novels, and films.

To wield this weapon Gribanov created a new "14th Department" within his internal-counterintelligence directorate and gave it the mission of "mounting complicated counterintelligence operations and operational games to penetrate foreign intelligence services." He would direct it personally, but installed as its chief his principal assistant during their investigation and interrogation of Popov, Colonel Valentin Zvezdenkov. Together they set out to hand CIA yet another high GRU officer, but this time their own. He would re-use Popov's information (and a bit more) to win CIA's trust and in the best tradition of nastupatelnost' would expose it, lead it astray, and draw its officers into compromising situations.

Gribanov's 14th Department (and other KGB components) did it time and again, from within both GRU and KGB. General Sergey Kondrashev spoke after the Cold War of "repeated" proposals for such operations in his own FCD disinformation unit. He himself had been invited to shift over to the SCD to help Gribanov run the Nosenko provocation. Another KGB veteran even said (likely with a degree of hyperbole) that "most" of the CIA spies inside the KGB who were betrayed by CIA traitor Aldrich Ames in 1985 were in fact loyal staffers pretending to help CIA.

For this particular enterprise Gribanov and Zvezdenkov chose GRU Lieutenant Colonel Dmitry Polyakov.[1] As a first step they dispatched him in October 1959 to New York, where he had already served in the past, as a military functionary in the Soviet delegation to the United Nations. It was not truly launched until two years later, however, because Polyakov had first to establish himself in his cover position and then because Gribanov delayed the operation while dealing with an unexpected complication. Having discovered a new, real traitor within the GRU, Colonel Oleg Penkovsky (see next section), Gribanov had to weigh the effects on his planned operation. So it was not until the fall of 1961 after safely "cornering [Penkovsky] like a bear in its den" that Gribanov felt ready to launch the operation.

As Jim F. told a close colleague on the operation, who told me in 1970. Polyakov asked an American military officer to put him in touch with CIA. The FBI made the contact, it being their jurisdiction, and for several months they met him secretly in New York (codenaming him "Tophat"). Enthusiastic at the time about what Polyakov was revealing, fifteen years later the FBI looked back and wondered whether Polyakov had been deceiving them during those months. He had wasted their time on useless trails and nothing he had told them had importantly damaged the Soviet Union beyond what Popov had earlier reported.

After a few months Polyakov returned to Russia in the fall of 1962 and was not heard from until years later, when he told via a Moscow dead drop, that he would soon come out again. He came in 1966 as Soviet military attaché and GRU chief in Rangoon, Burma. Because operations abroad are the CIA's jurisdiction, the FBI soon turned over contact to CIA which continued to meet Polyakov in Burma from then until his tour of duty expired in 1969.

In his early meetings with Polyakov, the CIA case officer Jim F. had the strong impression that he was dealing with a KGB plant, but after a time he noted such dramatic improvement in the reporting that he became convinced that Polyakov was genuinely cooperating.

For years thereafter Polyakov continued direct and indirect contacts with CIA, turning over priceless military and intelligence secrets first in Rangoon, then in Moscow, and then in two separate tours of duty in New Delhi where he enjoyed the rank of one-star general, making him the highest-ranked secret source that CIA ever had in Soviet Russia.

But then in May 1980 the operation came to an abrupt end. On the pretext of a supposed meeting of military attaches, Polyakov was recalled to Moscow and never heard from again.

Ten years later in 1990, out of the blue, the Soviets announced that they had arrested Polyakov, tried him in secret for being a CIA spy, and executed him Their publicity chose to date the arrest as 1986, the trial and execution as March 1988. It took another dozen years to begin explaining these oddities -- the secret trial so unlike Penkovsky's, the lack of even a fuzzy explanation of how the KGB had caught Polyakov, the inexplicable dates and unusual publicity.

The only KGB foreign-operations officer who had known of the SCD's operation, General Sergey Kondrashev (who had been that KGB deputy for disinformation mentioned above), revealed to me that Gribanov had sent Polyakov out in the first place.

"But they executed Polyakov!" I said. "Why would the KGB execute a man whom they themselves had sent out to commit this treason?"

"Because they found out he was giving you more than he was supposed to."

"Found out? How?"

Kondrashev answered: "Through some source inside American Intelligence."

He would say no more. But the question hung there: Who could have known exactly how much Polyakov was reporting to CIA? It had to be someone inside CIA's Soviet operations staff. And someone still undiscovered. Two Americans who knew something of the Polyakov case were later discovered to have been traitors -- but neither of them could be the answer. Robert Hanssen of the FBI had told the Soviets in 1979 about Polyakov's 1962 cooperation in New York, but of course he knew nothing of what Polyakov later reported to CIA. And even in the unlikely event that CIA traitor Aldrich Ames had learned the full details of Polyakov's reporting, Ames did not begin betraying until 1985, five years after the KGB had recalled Polyakov on a ruse and terminated the operation.

Not one of the later-discovered CIA traitors could even remotely have been aware of these details. In fact, only a handful of specially-placed CIA operatives knew even that the Agency had a relationship with Polyakov, much less what Polyakov was reporting. In each report that CIA passed to military and other government agencies they disguised the source and attributed reports on different subjects to different sources.

The whole gamut of Polyakov's reporting could have been known only to his CIA handlers and those dealing with his raw reports. So the question hangs: Who told the KGB what Polyakov was telling CIA?

About The Author

Edward Jay Epstein is the author of 15 books, eight of which have been excerpted in The New Yorker, the Atlantic, and the Sunday Times of London. He received his Pd.D. from Harvard after receiving his master's degree in government from Cornell. His master's thesis on the search for political truth became the best-selling book "Inquest: The Warren Commission and the Establishment of Truth." His doctoral dissertation on television news was published as "News from Nowhere." He is the recipient of numerous foundation grants and awards, including the prestigious Financial Times/Booz Allen prize for both best biography and best business book for "Dossier: The Secret History of Armand Hammer."

His website is *www.edwardjayepstein.com*

Other Books by Edward Jay Epstein

Inquest
Legend
News from Nowhere
The Rise and Fall of Diamonds
Agency of Fear
Between Fact and Fiction
Dossier: Armand Hammer
The Big Picture
The Hollywood Economist
The Annals of Unsolved Crime

Short-Form Books

James Jesus Angleton: Was He Right?
The JFK Assassination Diary
Have You Ever Tried to Sell a Diamond?
Three Days in May: Sex, Videos and DSK
Myths of the Media
Armand Hammer: The Darker Side
The Rockefellers
Sixty Views of the Kennedy Assassination
Garrison's Game
Who Killed God's Banker
Crude Cartel
Tabloid America: Crimes of the Press
The Money Demons: True Fables of Wall Street

CPSIA information can be obtained at www.ICGtesting.com
Printed in the USA
LVOW10s1809170715

446653LV00004B/424/P